SOUTH BUTON AND THE "WOMB" OF EASTERN INDONESIAN ISLAM

By Caleb Coppenger

Copyright © 2020, Caleb Coppenger
First Edition

Without limiting the rights under copyright reserved above, no part of this publication may be reproduced, stored in or introduced into a retrieval system, or transmitted, in any form or by any means (electronic, mechanical, photocopying, recording, or otherwise), without the prior written permission of both the copyright owner and the publisher of this book.

Published by Aventine Press
55 E Emerson St.
Chula Vista CA 91911
www.aventinepress.com

ISBN: 978-1-59330-972-5

Library of Congress Control Number: 2020904716
Library of Congress Cataloging-in-Publication Data
South Buton and the "Womb" of Eastern Indonesian Islam

Printed in the United States of America

ALL RIGHTS RESERVED

Dedicated to Tiffany

The love of my life and partner in this journey
to the seventh level

TABLE OF CONTENTS

Preface	1
Introduction	5
I. The Fortresses and Islands of South Buton	19
II. The Rapid, Worldwide Spread of Islam	27
III. The Influence of Trade in the Spread of Islam	39
IV. The Portuguese and Ternate	47
V. The Influence of Sufism in the Spread of Islam	57
VI. Orthodox and Popular Sufism	67
VII. The Seven Levels (*Martabat Tujuh*)	75
VIII. Reformism and Traditionalism	85
IX. Mysticism on Buton	93
Bibliography	101
Significant Empires, Sultanates, Laws, & Brotherhoods	113
Glossary	115
Index	121

Maps

#1 Southeast Sulawesi Map	vi
#2 Empire & Caliphate Map	vii
#3 Southwest Asia Map	viii
#4 Southeast Asia Map	ix
#5 India Map	x

Note on maps: The cities, empires, and regions identified on these maps are to provide the reader a visual depiction of the geographic location of key historical places mentioned in the book within the current geopolitical landscape. In most cases the countries identified on the maps were not in existence during the timeframe that this book mentions the cities, empires, and regions, so the maps are not historically accurate.

Tables

#1 Sufi Levels of Being (pg.77)
#2 Sufi Realms of Being (pg.78)
#3 Societal Categories in Butonese Sultanate (pg.97)

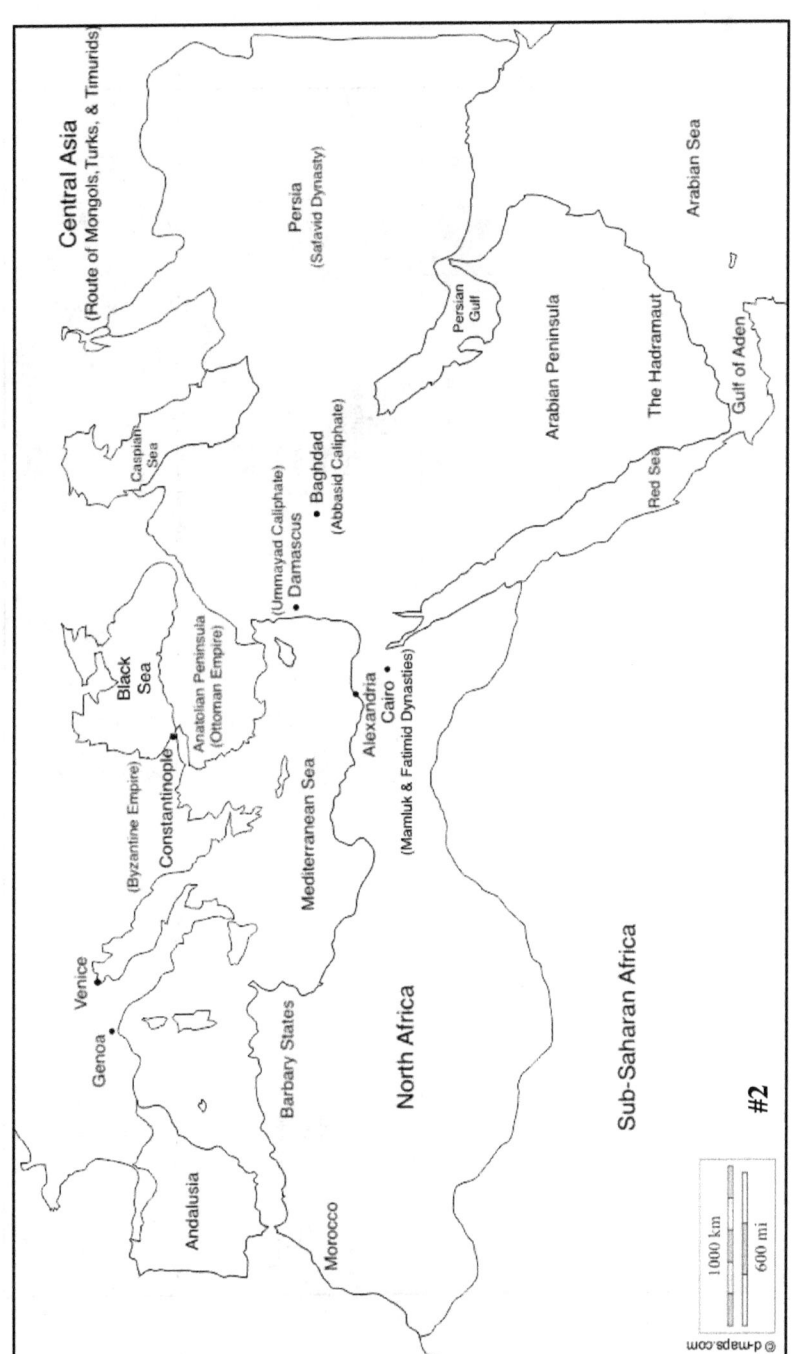

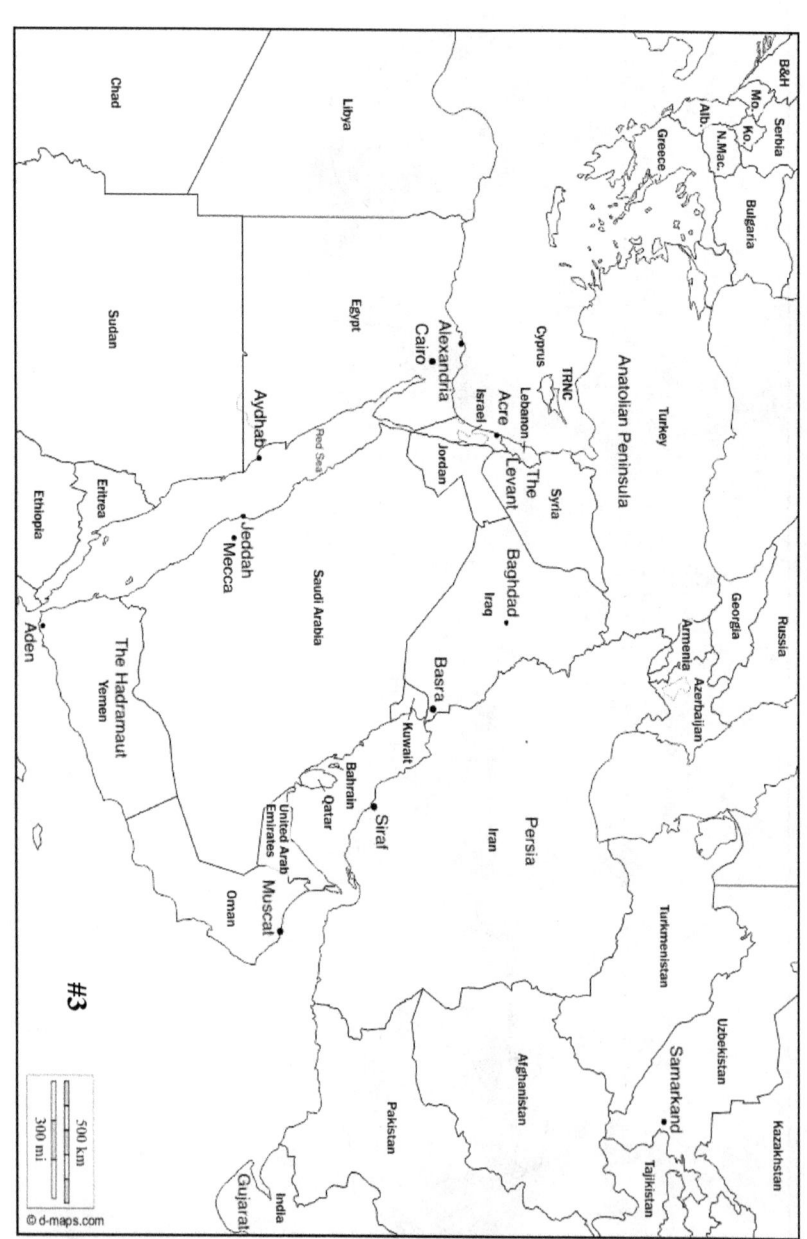

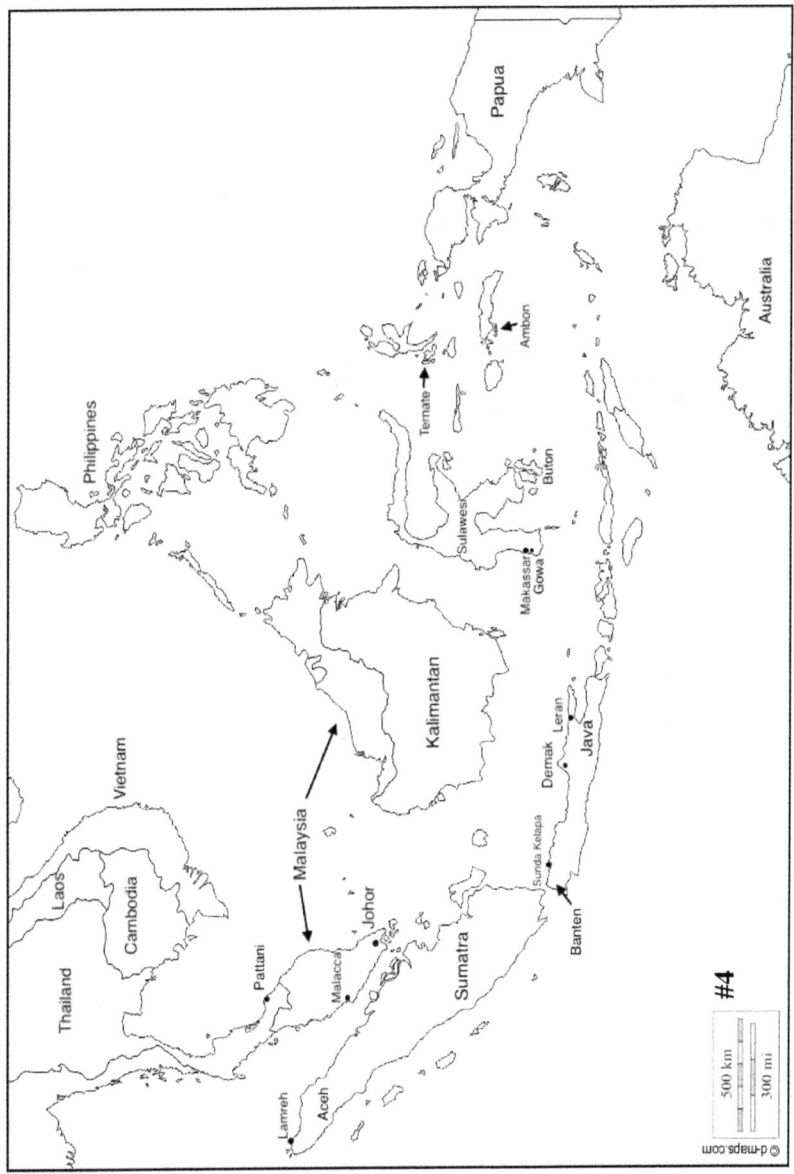

PREFACE

I have called Buton home for the past 12 years and have guided guests from the United States and Australia throughout the islands that were part of the former Kingdom, and later Sultanate, of Buton. Guests are always surprised at the hospitality of the Muslims that live on these islands, because most of the news about Islam in America is negative. It is refreshing for people from the West to meet and interact with Muslims in a positive way, but they are often confused as to how the Muslims on Buton seem so different from the Islam they have always learned about. They often consider the Islam that they have experienced on Buton as Folk Islam, and probably not an accurate depiction of "true Islam." This is unfortunate, because the people of Buton are very much "true Muslims" and have been since birth. The diversity of belief and practice throughout the Muslim world is not something new, but has been around since the 9th century. More recent reformist efforts have been underway for many years and usually dominate the public dialogue on Islam. This book is being written for guests that come to visit Buton, so they can better understand the background and beliefs of the Muslims they regularly encounter.

There is very little of my own opinion in this book, but I have sought to compile information from a variety of sources that seem to ring true with my experience of living on Buton.

Recent works by Ahmed, Knysh, and Laffan have been especially helpful. I am not attempting to present a "true version" of Islam, because I myself am not a Muslim, but am an outsider that has grown to respect and care for the people that live on these islands. I haven't seen a good explanation of the type of Islam found on Buton for outsiders, so I have tried to create an understandable and accessible picture of Butonese Islam so that guests can better understand what they are seeing and not discount the Butonese as living outside the norms of Islam. The traditions of Islam are very broad and the vast majority of Butonese Muslims fall within these norms according to current and past scholarship on Islam.

I hope that this book is a positive contribution to a current understanding of Islam in Eastern Indonesia. I appreciate the careful reading and suggestions on the manuscript from my Mom, Dad, David Mead, and René van den Berg. I take responsibility for any errors in this book, and I apologize if the reader feels like Islam has been misrepresented in any way. There are a variety of differing views of Islam presented in this book, and in each case I have tried to provide the citation for where this information originated. I'm sure the authors of each of the sources cited in this book are willing to back up their statements with valid research and experience. This book should be considered a compilation of the current research and opinions on mysticism within Islam and how Islam spread from its place of origin in the Middle East all the way to Eastern Indonesia. My goal was to help provide a crucial first step in understanding Islam in Buton, but any deeper understanding will require direct interaction with the Muslims that live on Buton or have originated from this island. I do not claim to speak for them, they are more than able to speak for themselves.

This book gives significant focus to the southern portion of the island of Buton, especially within the borders of the South Buton Regency which was formed in 2014. South Buton has much to offer in terms of history, culture, and natural wonders.

"The Wonder of South Buton" was very appropriately chosen as the regency's tag line during their first major festival in 2019. This part of the island has also been identified as holding "1,000 mysteries," which is also true. There is still much to learn about South Buton, but I hope that this book will get the reader one step closer to understanding the tourism potential that this regency has to offer. It has been a joy to live in Buton these past 12 years and the hospitality of the Butonese people has been a blessing to my family and the guests that have come to visit. Come and experience the culture, mystery, and wonder of South Buton!

INTRODUCTION

The Island of Buton in Eastern Indonesia has generally been known as a place that people pass through on their way to the Spice Islands to the east, or on the return trip to the city of Makassar to the west. Not many people set their sights on Buton as a final destination, unless exiled there from some larger kingdom. But the people originating from the islands of Buton call it home, and they have pride in the community they have built among its villages and throughout the smaller surrounding islands. It was no small task to develop this sense of unity as "people of Buton" because of the multitude of people groups and languages dwelling in these lands. The Butonese have also had freedom to live and worship as they see fit, since no one has been overly interested in doing the hard work of colonizing these islands, which are small and hard to manage. This has allowed Buton to preserve Islam in a state very similar to how it was brought to them hundreds of years ago.

At the turn of the twenty-first century there were approximately 1.2 billion Muslims worldwide, with most of the major population centers located in Asia and the top five largest Muslim national populations located outside of the Arab Middle East. Today nearly 60 percent of the Muslims living in the world do so in Asia. By comparison, the combined populations of all of the Arabic-speaking Muslim nations of the Middle East add up to less than 20 percent of today's global *umma*.[1] As Feener notes, "The focus on complex and multi-vectored interactions, both historical and contemporary, between Muslim societies in South and Southeast Asia, should not be simply about highlighting one alternative region of the Muslim world over another, but rather of reflecting upon demographic realities as a means of stimulating new ways of approaching the study of Muslim societies." Some analogous movements are underway among those who study "global Christianity."[2] Just as studies of Christianity today should not necessarily be focused on the West, studies on Islam today should not necessarily be focused on the Middle East.

The past hundred years or so have seen major changes in the way that Islam is understood throughout the world, by both its adherents and outsiders. There has been a reformation of sorts in an effort to discern the local beliefs and cultures that have marked Islam since it spread east and west from the Arabian Peninsula, analyzing adjustments that have made it palatable to a diverse range of people and locations.[3] On one hand, many have sought to conform faithful Muslims to a version of Islam "more suited" to the modern world. On the other, some have tried to re-create the early years of Islam, and these two versions are essentially polar opposites.

Modernist Reformist

The modern version of Islam seeks to show how the faith is not outdated, and is just as legitimate as the other world religions—a belief system that people can embrace with pride, even with advanced degrees and from places of prominence in

---
[1] R. Michael Feener, "Issues and Ideologies in the Study of Regional Muslim Cultures" in Feener, *Connections*, xiii.
[2] Ibid., xix.
[3] Martin van Bruinessen, ed., *Contemporary Developments in Indonesian Islam: Explaining the "Conservative Turn"* (Singapore: Institute of Southeast Asian Studies (ISEAS), 2013), 1-20.

the world. This modernist version is popular among the civil servants and more formally educated people of Indonesia, people who are conservative enough to still believe that the teachings of Islam hold authority over their lives, but who are sensitive to the modern sense that the mysticism and local cultural beliefs which have attached themselves to Islam are outdated and somewhat embarrassing.[4] On this model, many of the legal traditions and more formal aspects of Islam that have developed over the last one thousand years are still accepted. The organization in Indonesia today that best represents this position is Muhammadiyah.

Muhammadiyah was founded in 1912 with a modernist vision for combining spiritual and intellectual reform with practical innovations in education and health care inspired by the modernist ideas of Muhammad Abduh in Cairo.[5] The vast majority of modernists in Indonesia are associated with Muhammadiyah, which is thought to have 30 million members widely distributed throughout the country, with strong support in Sumatra, Sulawesi and Java. The Islamic influence of the Arab countries on Indonesia initially came through contact with Mecca, but since 1930 Cairo has come to the forefront. Muhammad Abduh and his successor, Rashid Rida, are still honored in Indonesia as the great reformers of Islam in this age, and there is still a close relationship between Indonesian Muslims and Al-Azhar in Cairo. K.H. Ahmad Dahlan, the founder of Muhammadiyah in 1912, is generally considered the great reformer of Islam in Indonesia.[6] Muhammadiyah has established its own network of educational institutions, hospitals, and orphanages, and seeks to meet important social needs and

---

[4] Pieternella van Doorn-Harder, *Women Shaping Islam: Indonesian Women Reading the Quran* (Urbana: University of Illinois Press, 2006), 51.

[5] Greg Barton, "Islam and Democratic Transition in Indonesia" in Tun-Jen Cheng and Deborah A. Brown, eds., *Religious Organizations and Democratization: Case Studies from Contemporary Asia* (Armonk: M.E. Sharpe, Inc., 2006), 225.

[6] J. Boland, *The Struggle of Islam in Modern Indonesia* (The Hague: Martinus Nijhoff, 1971), 212-215.

to spread the reformist message. The goals of Muhammadiyah include simultaneously simplifying and eliminating non-Islamic elements from rituals and ceremonies.[7] Traditional Indonesian folk practices such as the widespread ritualization of death in the form of communal feasts, pilgrimage to graves of local saints, consultation of fortune tellers, and the use of black magic are strictly rejected as expressions of superstition (*takhyul*) and polytheism (*syirik*).[8] The last century has seen growth in Islamic reformist movements, but some are more radical than others.

Salafi

The versions of Islam that glorify the early years of the religion centered on the Arabian Peninsula are what have caused so much negative publicity for Islam today, and are generally referred to as *Salafi* (meaning "ancestors"). Instead of believing that Islam just needs to be updated to the modern world to make it more effective as a belief system within which people and nations can thrive, they reject almost everything that has taken place within Islam beyond the first three generations of the faith.[9] These versions generally consider the legal traditions and history of Islam over the last one thousand years to have strayed from the original teachings, and its call for reform of Muslim belief and practice is partly by returning to the model of Muhammad and his companions.[10]. Indeed, these purists are

---

[7] Hajriyanto Y. Thohari, Fuad Fanani Ahmad, Andar Nubowo, and Muhd. Abdullah Darraz, *Becoming Muhammadiyah: Autobiografi Gerakan Kaum Islam Berkemajuan* (Bandung: Mizan, 2016), 92-93.

[8] Christian Kiem, "Re-Islamization among Muslim Youth in Ternate Town," in *Soujorn: Journal of Social Issues in Southeast Asia,"* Vol. 8, No. 1 (February 1993), 101-102.

[9] Lav, Daniel. *Radical Islam and the Revival of Medieval Theology.* Cambridge: Cambridge University Press, 2012.

[10] Bernard Haykel, "On the Nature of Salafi Thought and Action" in *Global Salafism: Islam's New Religious Movement* edited by Roel Meijer (New York: Columbia University Press, 2009), 33-34.

convinced that, in many cases, Muslims who differ with them are not "true Muslims" at all. Like the modernist versions, these Muslims also generally reject mysticism and local cultural beliefs, primarily because they are considered to be from man and not God. Even though mysticism has been a part of Islam from the beginning, it did not begin to flourish until after the initial military advance of Islam. *Salafi* Muslims look towards an era of Islam that predates the proliferation of mystical Islamic beliefs to and from other cultures.[11]

Traditionalism

The middle road between these two versions of Islam is what I would argue is still the majority view of Muslims throughout the world in the way that they live their lives. Nevertheless, it's the view that the adherents are least capable of defending and sharing with others.[12] In most cases it contains aspects that are unique to a certain culture or geographic location, so does not apply universally. Still, it shares manifestations with other areas. It is usually identified as traditionalism. This position also accepts mysticism as an important part of Islam, even though, today, the modern and ancient versions of Islam both reject mysticism for different reasons.[13] The people that hold to this more centrist view of Islam are also usually less educated (in a formal sense, which in no way reflects their intelligence), and they follow the faith as it is passed down from their parents and

---

[11] Andree Feillard and Remy Madinier, *The End of Innocence? Indonesian Islam and the Temptations of Radicalism* (Singapore: National University of Singapore Press in association with IRASEC (a French Research Institute on Contemporary Southeast Asia), 2011).

[12] D. Palmer, "Trading Traditions: Modernist Islam and Agricultural Rituals in Buton, Indonesia," in *Faith in the future: understanding the revitalization of religions and cultural traditions in Asia* edited by Thomas Reuter & Alexander Horstmann (Leiden: Brill, 2013), 207-212.

[13] Alexander Knysh, *Sufism: A New History of Islamic Mysticism* (Princeton: Princeton University Press, 2017), 1-14.

grandparents. They don't arrive at their practice as the result of extended study or radical obedience to God, but rather as a result of being raised in an Islamic community. It's the version of Islam that rarely has a voice today, and the version that I would argue can be seen more clearly in Buton than in other areas because of its relative isolation and the large variety of people groups and languages that need to live in harmony.

The organization in Indonesia most closely related to the traditionalist position is Nahdlatul Ulama (NU), which is very popular in Indonesia. But the organization is not very well regulated, so membership numbers of 40 million are probably not very exact. NU is rooted in the mystical, Sufi-flavored Islam seen throughout Indonesia. These traditionalist Muslims in Indonesia reject both the reformist Islam of Muhammadiyah and the spread of Westernization as they are both thought to lead to secularization and a loss of cultural identity. What reformists may regard as pre-Islamic *adat*, members of NU view as local versions of Islam.[14] Throughout Indonesia the customary law of *adat* plays a powerful role in the practices, norms, and claims about social life that draw their force not from scripture, nor from a positive-law-like process of enactment, but from their source in the local community's past.[15] NU defends the form of Islamic teaching and practice that recognizes the authority of the four *madhhab* (the orthodox schools of law), the charismatic authority of a *shaykh*, the importance of visiting holy graves, and the validity of Sufi ethics and ritual.[16] The organization *Jam'iyah Ahlith Thariqah Mu'tabarah An-Nahdliyah* (JATMN) is also a specifically Sufi organization officially affiliated with

---

[14] Kiem, 104.
[15] John R. Bowen, *Islam, Law and Equality in Indonesia: An Anthropology of Public Reasoning* (Cambridge: Cambridge University Press, 2003), 29.
[16] Michael Laffan, "National Crisis and the Representation of traditional Sufism in Indonesia: The Periodicals *Salafy* and *Sufi*" in *Sufism and the 'Modern' in Islam* edited by Martin van Bruinessen and Julia Day Howell (New York: I.B. Tauris & Co Ltd, 2007), 149.

NU.[17] NU is primarily focused on the island of Java, but it is a significant representative of traditionalist Islam throughout Indonesia. NU has dared to draw a line between ideology and religion, and openly embraced nationalist ideals. This "liberation of Islam from political stigma and constraints" has resulted in a "reduction of suspicion" on the part of the government and the initiation of programs designed to increase Islamic influence in national culture.[18]

One can deduce from looking at the current population of Indonesia that it is considered legitimate to be a devout Muslim without associating oneself with an Islamic organization, which most Muslims choose to do. Indonesians have also been historically categorized, especially in Java, as *santri*, "orthodox" Muslims, and *abangan*, "signifying those who are nominally Muslims but have little knowledge of their religion. These terms do not imply that *abangan* represents "heterodox" Muslims, but that they know less about Islam, are not overly concerned with its precepts, and so are not very strict in fulfilling their religious obligations."[19] Traditionalism within Indonesia is usually identified with the variety of popular expressions of Islam referred to as Sufism or Folk Islam, which involve visiting shrines of Muslim saints and an aversion to political and puritan styles of Islam. This category could also include those with tendencies toward Javanese mystical syncretism, known as *kebatinan*.[20] This overview of general categories of Muslims in

---

[17] Bruinessen, *Conservative*, 52-53.
[18] Andree Feillard, "Traditionalist Islam and the State in Indonesia: The Road to Legitimacy and Renewal" in *Islam in an Era of Nation-States: Politics and Religious Renewal in Muslim Southeast Asia* edited by Robert W. Hefner and Patricia Horvatich (Honolulu: University of Hawai'i Press, 1997), 149-150.
[19] Fauzan Saleh, *Modern Trends in Islamic Theological Discourse in 20th Century Indonesia: A Critical Survey* (Leiden: Brill, 2001), 97-98.
[20] Martin van Bruinessen, "Sufism, 'Popular' Islam and the Encounter with Modernity," in *Islam and Modernity: Key Issues and Debates*, edited by Muhammad Khalid Masud, Armando Salvatore, and Martin van Bruinessen (Edinburgh: Edinburgh University Press, 2009), 145-149.

Indonesia should be helpful in starting to understand the current state of Islam today before we start to look farther back in history.

To understand the origin of the Islam of Buton, we will need to look at how it was brought to the island, and how it was accepted by the Kingdom that ruled at the time. This background is key to understanding what aspects of Islam in Buton today are similar to those that were taught when it was first accepted in the mid-1500's. Mysticism was a key part of the indigenous belief system, and was even codified in the manuscripts and the structure of the Sultanate, the proof still existing today.[21] This mysticism is also still very much a part of how the people think and make decisions on how to be a faithful Muslim in the modern world. This middle road version of Islam has kept the peace in this area for a long time and can provide a starting point for understanding what Islam looked like in many places throughout the world before reform efforts created so much controversy and conflict today over what is "truly Islamic." It also played an important role in the acceptance of Islam throughout the islands of Indonesia.

The Spread of Islam

The spread of Islam in Southeast Asia is similar to that of mainland Asia in that there is no one explanation that is sufficient, but a variety of factors. This is true throughout the Islamic world where differences usually derive both from the different pre-existing cultural backgrounds and the nature of the early Islamic missionaries.[22] "Major speculations and controversies have revolved around the possible source of Indonesian Islam (Arabia, North and South India, Persia, China, and Kurdistan have all been suggested), the dating of its arrival, the chronology

---

[21] Abd. Rahim Yunus, *Posisi Tasawuf Dalam Sistem Kekuasaan di Kesultanan Buton Pada Abad Ke-19* (Jakarta: INIS, 1995).

[22] J. Spencer Trimingham, *The Sufi Orders in Islam* (London: Oxford University Press, 1971), 131.

of the unfolding process, and the reasons for a major Islamization occurring only several centuries after Muslims are known to have been present in the region."[23] There are generally four factors that led to the Islamization of Southeast Asia: Arab merchants, 'pilgrims of learning', preachers, and the *hajj*.[24] The preachers and some 'pilgrims of learning' that traveled abroad and brought their teaching back to Indonesia and Malaysia, often taught Islam that was mystical (or Sufi) in nature. Another major factor in the spread of Islam to Indonesia was the prevalence of Sufi literature and its wide dissemination. It should also be emphasized that Jawi scholars (Malay individuals) played a major role in Islamization, and it was not just those from outside the area such as Arabs and Indians.[25] The development of Sufi teaching that gained prominence during the Abbasid Empire moved east. The Abbasid Empire, centered in Baghdad, Iraq (750-1258 AD) was one of the first and most successful Islamic Empires, was heavily influenced by Persia, and was not primarily administered by Arabs. Even though the Middle East is where Islam originated, it took on a life of its own as it gained more followers. Sufism has been closely tied to mysticism throughout Islamic history.

The term "Sufism" was first used in Baghdad in the mid-ninth century, though was later used to describe similar practices that arose in other areas around the same timeframe, notably Basra in Southern Iraq, and Khurasan in Central Asia. In the eighth and the first half of the ninth century "Sufi" referred to mystics commonly viewed as "radical renunciants," who often wore wool (Arabic *suf*) as a sign of their asceticism.

---

[23] Ronit Ricci, *Islam Translated: Literature, Conversion, and the Arabic Cosmopolis of South and Southeast Asia* (Chicago: The University of Chicago Press, 2011), 5, footnote 3.
[24] Peter G. Riddell, "Arab Migrants and Islamization in the Malay World during the Colonial Period," in *Indonesia and the Malay World*, Vol. 29, No. 84 (2001), 113.
[25] Michael Laffan, *The Makings of Indonesian Islam: Orientalism and the Narration of a Sufi Past* (Princeton: Princeton University Press, 2011), 18.

However, from the middle of the ninth century the term Sufi was increasingly used as "a technical term to designate a group of people who belonged to a clearly identifiable social movement in Baghdad that was based on a distinct type of piety."[26] The first Sufis distanced themselves from the ascetics and were engaged in the world.[27] Practically all of the important developments in Sufism's early history are geographically related to greater Persia (including Mesopotamia), and many of the great figures of Sufism were ethnically Persian, though they wrote in Arabic.[28] Scholarship and adherence to Islamic law was a Sufi concern from the beginning, though there were challenges. Several Sufis made a reputation for themselves by uttering seemingly heretical and inflammatory remarks which led to their persecution by traditional preachers of Islam.[29]

The Sufis of Baghdad in the 9th century began to build on the concept growing in the Islamic world that individuals could be known as *awliya* or "friends of God." This was a status granted to only a few, those that had been elected by God. They had come to understand "the path to achieving proximity to the Creator (*tariqa*)," and rejected the idea that authority in Islam lay with the jurists who interpreted the law, but did not experience closeness to God. Some jurists viewed the Sufis with curiosity, some with contempt, and the Sufis generally did not help the situation by acting antagonistically toward the jurists.[30] During the 9th century there was a tug-of-war going on among Muslims

---

[26] Ahmet T. Karamustafa, *Sufism: The Formative Period* (Edinburgh: Edinburgh University Press, 2007), 6-7.

[27] Eric Geoffroy, *Introduction to Sufism: The Inner Path of Islam* (Bloomington: World Wisdom, 2010), 30.

[28] Seyyed Hossein Nasr, "The Rise and Development of Persian Sufism," in *Heritage of Sufism: Classical Persian Sufism from its Origins to Rumi (700-1300)*, Vol. 1, edited by Leonard Lewisohn (Oxford: Oneworld Publications, 1999), 2-3.

[29] Karamustafa, 11-12.

[30] Ibid., 19-22.

for who could claim special authority, and Sufi masters often felt themselves the most qualified.[31]

The friends of God were inferior to the prophets, but shared many similar characteristics with them. They claimed to know the secret meaning of the shapes of Arabic letters, they could travel great distances with great speed, and some claimed to walk on water. These supernatural acts were referred to as *keramat*, and were distinct from the term used for miracles of the prophets, *mukjizat*.[32] Apart from these displays of power, the core of Sufism was its focus on the inner self and achieving closeness to God. This was accomplished by becoming privy to secret knowledge held by the Sufi masters, as well as sessions of singing and worshiping together known as *sama*, which frequently resulted in one reaching a state of ecstatic fervor, *dhikr*, which would be a reminder of God's closeness. Sufis at this time were generally not celibate renunciants, but lived and sometimes worked in urban areas.

Sufism and authoritative Islam have historically found themselves and their doctrines in opposition to each other "only when they misunderstood each other, or when there was a conflict of authority, with one criticizing the other in order to keep control of its own flock."[33] Sufism has been an important part of Islam since the 9th century and some of the most important written works in Islam since that time have been by Sufis. "Sufism is a mystical tradition which, when compared to Christian and European institutions, could be put somewhere between monasticism and Freemasonry."[34] Sufism is notoriously hard to control and certain brotherhoods within Sufism in the past have been strong enough to seriously challenge the ruling establishment. The problem with the term "Sufi" today is that

---

[31] Ibid., 40.
[32] Ibid., 46.
[33] Geoffroy, 32.
[34] Julian Baldick, *Mystical Islam: An Introduction to Sufism* (London: I.B. Tauris and Co. Ltd., 1989), 3.

it has often come to encompass everything that does not strictly line up with what most of those in Islamic religious authority declare as normative. It may be helpful to categorize ancient local cultural practices from ethnic groups throughout the Islamic world that have been incorporated with the local expression of Islam today as Popular Sufism, as opposed to orthodox or normative Sufism. But one thing is clear, Sufism did not arise out of folk Islam.[35] While Islam's ability to mesh with local cultures is very much a part of Islamic history and practice, Sufism also has core theological characteristics that transcend individual cultures and are seen throughout the Muslim world.[36] They are very much a part of mainstream Islam today and have been for centuries, with mystical teachings still alive and well in Eastern Indonesia.

Buton was on one of the major east-west trade routes within the archipelago that is now known as Indonesia. As the part of Buton that people would see when traveling between the Spice Islands and Makassar, South Buton has always been a prominent gateway to the island. Even though the largest city on the island, Baubau—historically the seat of the Sultanate of Buton—is located a little farther north, the story of Islam on Buton started on a little beach called *Rampea*, which means "run aground." The man that brought Islam to Buton was named Sheik Abdul Wahid, and his boat ran aground on this beach, and he is said to have established the first mosque on the island after seeing a light touch down at Wawoangi on his way to see the King of Buton. Not much is known about him on a personal level, except that which can be gathered locally on Buton through stories and traditions that have been passed down. Still, there are clues about the nature of the Islamic teachings he brought.

---

[35] Bernd Radtke and John O'Kane, *The Concept of Sainthood in Early Islamic Mysticism: Two works by Al-Hakim Al-Tirmidhi* (Surrey: Curzon Press, 1996), 7.

[36] Abdul Kadir Riyadi, *Arkeologi Tasawuf: Melacak Jejak Pemikiran Tasawuf dari Al-Muhasibi hingga Tasawuf Nusantara* (Bandung: Mizan, 2016), 355-358.

One way that Sufi Brotherhoods ensured their teachings stayed true to their founder was through detailed genealogies of their teachers (or sheiks), who passed down the teachings that usually are said to have originated from Muhammad. These are called *silsilah*, and it seems that Sheik Abdul Wahid received his teachings from another Sheik, who was part of the Sultanate of Johor or Pataani in current day Malaysia and South Thailand, respectively.[37]

This group of teachers from Johor spent long periods of time in Mecca, but, while they were there, they usually gathered with other ethnically Malay Muslims. Mecca is seen as the source of Islamic authority, but Al Azhar University in Cairo also has a prominent authoritative role for Sunni Muslims from the *Shafi'i* school of jurisprudence, honored by the vast majority of Muslims in Southeast Asia. (The Islam found in Saudi Arabia follows a different school of jurisprudence, *Hanbali*.) So even though many of these sheiks went to the Middle East for their training, they typically spent the majority of their time with people who spoke their same language and had a similar culture. This is one way Islam has taken on so many different characteristics in different regions.

India was also influential on Malay-Indonesian Islam because they were both in Asia, and many of the writings of Indian sheiks were more readily available (and had more of an Asian flair) than writings from Egypt and Saudi Arabia. Prominent sheiks from several of the Sufi brotherhoods were found in India, the Malay Peninsula, and throughout the Indonesian archipelago. By understanding what these sheiks passed on to Islam in Eastern Indonesia, we can better understand the Islam that is found on Buton. We will first look at the southern coast of Buton where Islam first arrived on the island, followed by tracing the path of

---

[37] Azyumardi Azra, *The Origins of Islamic Reformism in Southeast Asia: Networks of Malay-Indonesian and Middle Eastern 'Ulama' in the Seventeenth and Eighteenth Centuries* (Honolulu: University of Hawai'i Press, 2004), 122-126.

Islam from the Middle East to East Indonesia through trade and Sufi teachers. Finally we will learn about the mystical aspects of Islam and how they have been preserved in the "womb" that is Buton.

I

THE FORTRESSES AND ISLANDS OF SOUTH BUTON

As seafarers traveled east from Sumatra, Java, and the largest city in Eastern Indonesia, Makassar, and entered the Banda Sea, they would pass by the southern end of the island of Buton. For those heading north to Ternate and the Malukus it would be possible to pass through the Tiworo islands on the west side of the island of Muna, or through the Buton Strait between Muna and Buton, but these chokepoints would leave little room to maneuver against pirates and others that might want to seize cargo. Most ships heading to Ternate, Ambon, and Papua would pass right by South Buton and the islands that make up this newly formed Regency in Southeast Sulawesi. The mystery and diversity of the island of Buton is well known, and South Buton is well positioned as a gateway to understanding the origin of many of the mysteries of the island, as well as experiencing its rugged beauty. It was the gateway through which Islam entered the island of Buton, and its fortresses and islands hold great potential for tourism in the Regency.

The limestone that forms the cliffs and hills of South Buton provided plenty of rocks with which to build fortresses to protect its inhabitants from invaders. Many of the villagers that relied on the sea for their livelihood also had a fortress they could run to when their shores were invaded by pirates or opposing kingdoms in their quests for slaves. Villages such as Burangasi, Lapandewa, Bahari, and Wawoangi have fortresses that still stand today and have provided a place to stand against invaders for centuries, as well as a place to conduct annual rituals and ceremonies. Some of these fortresses are still inhabited with houses now continuing outside their walls as a testament to population growth in the village. Other fortresses are at the top of high hills that can be explored by those ready for a hike, but they are no longer inhabited. Many of these fortresses also provided panoramic overlooks useful as lookout points for any threats from the sea. Geotourism trips to Buton should include a look at the limestone cliffs and fortresses most prominently displayed on the southern coast of Buton.

South Buton also holds some of the islands best suited for scuba diving surrounding the island of Buton. Batuatas is located about 50 kilometers to the south of Buton, isolated from the other islands of the province. This geographic isolation and deep surrounding waters provide some of the best scuba diving in the province, especially surrounding the shallow reef located about an hour's boat ride from the island known as Manaa. The islands of Siompu, Liwotongkidi (or Snake Island), and Kadatua are closer to the cities of Batauga and Baubau and also offer excellent diving. The fortresses and people of Batuatas, Siompu, and Kadatua also harbor rich cultures and are always excited when tourists come to visit. Siompu is especially desirable because of several freshwater springs pouring out of the island near the coastline where guests can wash off after a saltwater swim, and when its oranges are in season. There are many small islands in Southeast Sulawesi, but the reefs and pinnacles surrounding the islands of Batuatas, Kadatua, and Siompu in South Buton are probably the only ones that rival the scuba diving in Wakatobi.

In addition to these natural attractions that would be enough to draw any adventurous ecotourists to the island, the history of Buton starts in the south. One origin myth tells of a Chinese man named Teweke that landed by boat on the southeastern shore of the island, near Wabula, after following the vision of a woman who appeared to him as a bright light.[38] A woman of Chinese or Mongolian descent named Wakaakaa has also been associated with this boat and is said to have been the first queen, but other stories say she emerged from a shoot of bamboo. As with most of these stories, there are usually several versions depending on who is asked. Wakaakaa and other individuals related to the founding of the Kingdom of Buton are pre-Islam. In the village of Lapandewa in South Buton, the story goes that the traditional founder of the kingdom, Sipanjonga, landed in Lakaliba (near Gaya Baru) originally with his three companions, and eventually married a woman in Lapandewa. The fortress in Lapandewa is connected to the fortress in Baubau that was the seat of the Kingdom of Buton through sibling relationships. The person named Sipanjonga is usually referred to in the story told in Baubau, but in Lapandewa the story is a little different.

According to the Lapandewa tradition, there were two brothers, Labukuterinde who lived in Lapandewa, and Labaluwu who lived closer to Baubau. Labukuterinde presided over the fortress in Lapandewa, and Labaluwu was one of several individuals that established the kingdom in Baubau. Labukuterinde was told by his mother when he was younger that he had a brother, and she gave him half of a coconut shell and told him that his long-lost brother had the other half of the shell. If he ever found a man that carried the other half of the shell, that man was his brother. Labukuterinde was out hunting north of Lapandewa, and he came across a man named Labaluwu who was tapping toddy from sugar palms (*kanau*). Their initial meeting resulted in a fight, where they fought until they were both so exhausted that they considered the confrontation a draw.

---

[38] Michael Southon, "The navel of the perahu: meaning and values in the maritime trading economy of a Butonese village" (Master's Thesis, Australian National University, 1994), 16-17.

As they rested one of the men noticed the other man was carrying something and asked what it was. It was half of a coconut shell, and the other man produced the coconut shell half he had been carrying, and when they placed them together, they were a perfect fit. These two men then realized that they were brothers and they embraced. They decided to meet again on the southern coast in the Bay of Lande, and Labukuterinde came down from the hill of Lapandewa with some crops to give to Labaluwu, and Labaluwu came by boat from Baubau and brought some fish as his gift to Labukuterinde. This meeting is still commemorated each year in the village of Lande, as a goat is sacrificed there, and fish and rice are exchanged.[39] This sibling relationship between those of the fortress in Lapandewa and the fortress in Baubau is remembered by many in South Buton today, though it is not as well known in Baubau. The relationship between the seat of the former kingdom in Baubau and the other surrounding kingdoms during the pre-Islamic era is sometimes a source of contention today, particularly with the kingdom on the neighboring island and Regency of Muna. The arrival of the religion of Islam did play a role in unifying some of the smaller kingdoms on the islands of Southeast Sulawesi when it arrived in the 16th century.

The religion of Islam first came to the island after a boat ran aground near the village of Burangasi on the southern coast of Buton, in the current District of Lapandewa. These seafarers brought new ideas and information from faraway lands that Buton then proceeded to incorporate into their own cultures and beliefs. Islam had been developing and growing in other cultures for many years before it arrived on the shores of South Buton. Once Sheik Abdul Wahid arrived in South Buton, it would be some time before the Kingdom of Buton, based farther north in Baubau, adopted it as the religion of the kingdom. Even now, as modern reform efforts have not yet dominated the average villages of Buton, remnants of the Islam brought in the 16th

---

[39] Personal communication with a former Head of the Village of Lapandewa (November 2019).

century are still very prevalent. This makes for an invaluable resource for research conducted on the spread of mystical Islam to the islands of Indonesia. Of course, the Butonese story is but one of many, but the people of Buton consider their Islamic beliefs to have been preserved in a more pristine condition than others in the "womb" of Islam.

The name Buton is said to have come from the Arabic word *butn* or *bathni* or *bathin*, which means "stomach" or "womb." It's found in the old song *Kabanti Kanturuna Mohelana*. The story is that an Arab traveler was ordered by Muhammad to sail to the east to find an island that has long desired Islam, in order to preserve its true teachings. When he arrived, he placed his robe in a certain place on the island. This got the local inhabitant's attention, and they wondered who owned this robe. At one point, while looking at it, seven birds on the branch of a nearby tree[40] flew down one by one and said "butuni" each time. So the locals bowed down when they saw the owner of the robe who they considered to be "Waliullah," or "One sent by the Lord." From this term came the word "Wolio," which was applied to the former Sultanate of Buton in Baubau, as well as to the local people group and language that makes up the majority of the city.[41] Apart from this legend, the first report of a Muslim trader arriving in South Buton to try and win the island for Islam was Sheik Abdul Wahid in 1526. However it wasn't until 1541, when he returned with Imam Fathani, that the then king of Buton was inaugurated as a Sultan of the Sultanate of

---

[40] Another theory concerning the origin of the name Buton is that it comes from the name of the so-called sea poison tree, *Barringtonia asiatica* (L.) Kurz (which also gave its name to Bitung in North Sulawesi) (Kulisusu *bucu*, Wolio *butu*, etc. < Proto Malayo-Polynesian *|butun 'a shore tree: Barringtonia* spp.'). Naming places or even kingdoms after trees has a good bit of currency in Indonesia, including both Majapahit and Malacca. Nonetheless it in no way takes away from the *current* belief about Buton < *butuni* 'womb'." (Personal correspondence with the linguist David Mead on 25 Jan 2020).

[41] Abdul Mulku Zahari, *Katalog naskah Buton koleksi Abdul Mulku Zahari*, compiled by Achadiati Ikram (Yayasan Obor Indonesia, 2002), 2-3.

Buton, when Islam became the official religion. The complete name of this sheik was Abdul Wahid bin Syarif Sulaeman;[42] he identified with the teachings of al-Fathani and al-Juhuri.

The story goes that Sheik Abdul Wahid's boat ran aground on the small beach known as *Rampea* near Burangasi, and he began to walk east along the southern coast until he arrived at a rocky point on the coast known as *Matana Tai*, or the "eyes of the sea." This point is also known as *Tanjung Pomali* (or Forbidden Point), because of the blackish colored waters that are churning below the rocks and the eye-like rock formations that peer out from it. There were three local fisherman that happened to see the Sheik prostrated at this point and seemingly rocking back and forth and crying. This was the first reported time that someone prayed the Muslim *sholat* on the island, and the call to prayer uttered by Sheik Abdul Wahid sounded like he was crying with a loud voice. The local fishermen reported what they saw to the nearby village and along with the message that the Sheik came to bring the religion of Islam to the island. He was then escorted to nearby Sampolawa to the *kolaki* or *lakina* who had authority over the area. This *lakina* instructed the sheik to report directly to King Murhum of Buton. On his way to Baubau, around noon he was about to pass a place called Wawoangi, and decided to *sholat Zuhur* at that location. The significance of this noon prayer at this location led to the establishment of the first mosque on the island. The rest of the story of how King Murhum became the first Sultan after accepting Islam for the kingdom is best told from the viewpoint of the seat of the former Sultanate in Baubau, but the focus of this book is the nature of how Islam arrived on the island and would continue to influence it until the present day.

A short summary of the status of the first mosque on the island has circulated around Buton up to the present time:

---

[42] Yunus, *Tasawuf*, 19.

"Masjid Wawoangi was built by Syekh Abdul Wahid in 1527 in Sampolawa. He saw a light at this location, which means "above the wind." There are some graves around the mosque, including the father of the 7th Sultan of Buton, La Saparagau. The mosque is usually not used for *sholat*, because it is far from the village, but it is used for some cultural events. At one point, they renovated the roof with *sirap* (small boards from cheaper wood), but a local man was possessed by an ancestor who led them to change the roof back to one made of teak, like it was originally."[43]

This may sound like isolated "Folk Islam," full of superstition and mysticism that has strayed far from the original teachings of Islam, but the story is much more complicated than that. Stories of sheiks, strange lights, wind, graves, trances, and ancestors has been with Islam in the Middle East from the beginning and followed its history as far west as Spain and east through Iran and India and on to Malaysia and Indonesia. This cannot be explained away as Folk Islam, because it is a large part of Islamic teachings that are found throughout the world. Buton is just a little more outspoken about its traditions and even incorporated this mysticism into the structure of its sultanate. Visitors to South Buton today can see key places related to the initial birth of Islamic mysticism on the island of Buton that are still preserved in its "womb" until the present day, but in order to understand the big picture it is helpful to read about the worldwide development of Islamic mysticism and how it finally reached the shores of Buton in Eastern Indonesia.

---

[43] Description from La Ode Abdul Halim, Wawoangi Village Chief, in "Keunikan Masjid Wawoangi, Masjid Tertua di Pulau Buton," in IKONS, 19 June 2017, https://www.ikons.id/keunikan-masjid-wawoangi-masjid-tertua-di-pulau-buton/ (accessed on 18 Feb 2020).

II

THE RAPID, WORLDWIDE SPREAD OF ISLAM

The spread of Islam comes up frequently in discussions, because recent attacks in the name of jihad have driven people to look at its origins. Most of the time they go back to the rapid spread of Islam in its first few years and conclude that Islam is a religion that is primarily spread by the sword. They are also familiar with reports that countries with majority Muslim populations make it illegal to formally leave Islam, and that children born into families with Muslim parents have no choice over what religion they follow when they become adults. (Once a Muslim, always a Muslim, otherwise one is considered a traitor.) On the other hand, there are frequent references to a verse in the Quran saying, "there is no compulsion in religion." This usually doesn't satisfy, because actual events seem to say otherwise.

Islam has a long, complicated history, and a great deal happened in the millennium between the faith's first years and these last centuries. Saying that Islam spread by the sword and by coercion is only part of the story, and like most belief systems with millions of adherents there is no simple explanation. The majority of Muslims throughout history have been converted through much less sensational means. Most Muslims are not converts in the Malcolm X sense (after he left the Nation of

Islam), but, rather, they are raised in the faith and don't have a life-changing, "come to faith" moment. It's more like the air they breathe from the start, and back in medieval times conversion took place as a local ruler accepted the religion for personal or political reasons and all of his subjects then fell under the realm of Islam. This was similar to what happened with Christian Empires during the medieval era, but this method of allegiance at birth continues until the present day in the Islamic world. Adults and children have become Muslims in a variety of different settings and traditions, and the Islam that they ascribe to looks very different and is understood very differently, depending on the culture in which the Muslim lives. There are many examples throughout history to illustrate this, and they help to give a more complete picture of the true scope of Islam. By studying the expression and practice of Islam in different cultures throughout Islamic history, we find diversity and flexibility providing various pathways to conversion, even though current Islamic leadership usually tries to minimize these differences.

The Arab world, as the land where Islam began, is an appropriate place to start. This was primarily a tribal area, where it was traditionally difficult to convince the egalitarian tribes to work together.[44] With the arrival of someone who declared himself a prophet, tribal confederation became possible, and so began the spread of Islam in Medina. There were many factors other than Muhammad's report that he had received revelation from Allah that convinced people to follow him. There were also some political and economic issues at play, and the confederation's first move was to take revenge on those who rejected Muhammad in Mecca. From these humble beginnings there began a military advance that moved with amazing rapidity.

---

[44] Thomas J. Barfield, "Turk, Persian, and Arab: Changing Relationships between Tribes and State in Iran and along Its Frontiers," in *Iran and the Surrounding World: Interactions in Culture and Cultural Politics* edited by Nikki R. Keddie and Rudi Matthee (Seattle: University of Washington Press, 2002), 65-70.

There were clear instances where people were conquered and basically forced to convert to Islam through threats and pressure from an invading military force. At the same time, there were also reports of groups, such as the Jews, who had been so persecuted under the Byzantines that they welcomed the arrival of new leadership, even if they did not accept the new religion. There were Jews, Christians, and other groups of people who did not convert, and the caliph did not push the issue because the empire could collect the tax on these "second class citizens," *dhimmis*.[45] This may have led some to convert eventually for economic relief, as well as for other benefits from joining the religion of the empire.

The timing of the initial drive of Islam was crucial to its success. The Byzantine and Persian Empires had become very weak from constantly warring against each other, and, in the early 7th century, Muslim forces took advantage of the situation.[46] Not only had the weakened state of the empires made them less popular with the people; they also had trouble mustering enough forces to defend themselves. The Arabs were also able to gradually draw on the expertise that these two empires had developed in running their governmental affairs as officials left the declining empires and joined the new Islamic empire before their fortunes began to decline.[47]

The first Muslim dynasty, the Umayyad, which was centered in Damascus, was close enough to the former Byzantine capital that it probably employed many defectors in the management of its new empire. Islam had not only spread throughout the Arabian Peninsula, the Levant, and present-day Iraq, but it had overtaken northern Africa. Egypt was and continues to be the most important country in that area, but Morocco also has

---

[45] Mark Durie, *The Third Choice: Islam, Dhimmitude, and Freedom* (Deror Books, 2010).
[46] Efraim Karsh, *Islamic Imperialism: A History* (New Haven: Yale University Press, 2006), 21-26.
[47] Barfield, 71-72.

a proud heritage. Notably, the Berber people still retain their language and some of their own culture;[48] today they are the only significant group of Muslim non-Arabic speakers in North Africa. From Morocco, Muslim forces crossed over to Spain and easily took control of a portion of the Iberian Peninsula. Over time, the Umayyad Dynasty developed a bad reputation for its corrupt elites, and it was eventually overthrown. At least one prince from this dynasty was able to escape the failing dynasty in Damascus and make his way to Muslim controlled Spain, and his reign was followed by several smaller dynasties until Christian forces pushed them back to North Africa. The momentum of the Muslim advance was stopped in Eastern Europe under the leadership of Charles Martel near Poitiers/Tours in 732. Even though most of Europe resisted Islam on the continent, it enjoyed a reign of more than 700 years on the Iberian Peninsula (Spain and Portugal) from 711 to 1492.

Islam had again taken advantage of a weakly controlled situation in Spain, and once their government was established, they were very tolerant of the diversity in the area. For many years the Christians, Arabs and Berbers lived together in relative peace in Andalusia.[49] Wherever these invading Islamic forces conquered, it was usually in their best interest to show the locals that they would accommodate the local traditions and cultures. At this point, Islam was not fully developed as a religion, and its leadership lacked experience in running an empire. So the rulers often put local leaders in places of authority, granting them the titles and prestige needed to ensure that they would remain loyal. There is no doubt that these regional leaders used Islam to reinforce their legitimacy, but, in most cases, they were not Islamic holy men, and they may not have even adhered to the basic tenets of the faith. Most rulers of the era enjoyed absolute

---

[48] Clifford Geertz, *Islam Observed: Religious Development in Morocco and Indonesia* (New Haven: Yale University Press, 1968), 43-54.
[49] Thomas F. Glick, *Islamic and Christian Spain in the Early Middle Ages* (Princeton University Press, 1979).

power and their personal life and faith were not scrutinized by others. This same practice of using locals in administration was also employed in the east.

As the Umayyad dynasty came to an end in Damascus, it was replaced by the Abbasids, who chose Baghdad as their capital, which was fairly close to the capital of the former Persian Empire in Persepolis (near present-day Shiraz, Iran). This made it easy for the skilled Persian administrators to assist them. Their involvement was so significant that "one may surely say the Iranians played a dominant role in the development of the Abbasid bureaucracy, as well as in the creation of a universal Islamic culture."[50] Indeed, the involvement of the Persians had a great impact on Islam, specifically through the famous court of the caliphs that developed under the Abbasids and was one of the most cultured environments in the world at the time.[51] Like the Berbers, the Persians retained their language (Farsi), and because they were accustomed to operating as a hierarchal confederation of peoples, they brought stability to Islam that was difficult for the tribal Arabs.[52] It is also interesting to note that many of the classical exegetes of the Quran were Persian.[53]

Though the Persians underwent some Arabization because of conversion to Islam (with the only approved version of the Quran being in Arabic), Muslim leaders of the time were wise to allow cultural strengths to show through in spite of differences. Persian Islamic poetry is still studied today because of its beauty, along with miniature paintings[54] and other forms of cultural expression, such as the *Shahnameh* (a long epic poem of Greater Iran, the "Book of Kings"), which played an important role in

---

[50] Unknown, "Iranian Contributions to Islamic Culture," 155.
[51] Hugh Kennedy, *The Court of the Caliphs: The Rise and Fall of Islam's Greatest Dynasty* (London: Weidenfeld & Nicolson, 2004).
[52] Barfield, 65-70.
[53] Peter G. Riddell, *Islam and the Malay-Indonesian World: Transmission and Responses* (Honolulu: University of Hawai'i Press, 2001), 46.
[54] Stephen F. Dale, *The Muslim Empires of the Ottomans, Safavids, and Mughals* (New York: Cambridge University Press, 2010), 150.

the development of a national identity for modern Iran.[55] This willingness to learn from and work with the local leaders was crucial for Islam, and its reputation also drew scholars from the former Byzantine Empire, who brought their ideas with them.

With its cultural center in Baghdad, the Abbasid Empire was much influenced by Hellenistic rationalism, so philosophy and a culture of learning were specifically associated with the Abbasid Empire for a period of time. Once again, this was when Islam was still developing, and its leadership was being influenced by a large number of diverse cultures because of the vast empire it governed. Names such as Avicenna and Averroes are prominent from this time of rationalism, and their works are still read by Western philosophers today. But throughout history, this slow process of accretion, by which Islam was infused with regional cultures was challenged periodically by a reformist push to adhere to orthodox Islam, as understood by some Islamic scholars.[56] This reformism was usually connected with a ruler, who became fed up with the loose morals of Islamic leadership, and would impose harsh measures in an attempt to crush heretical practices. This was never completely successful, but it did give frequent rudder corrections to the far-flung kingdoms so Islam would have certain principles in common throughout the Islamic world. Hellenistic rationalism was eventually sidelined by the primacy of revelation, and change began to occur in the Islamic world as, several years later, the Mongols came in, destroyed the Abbasid caliphate, and took over. The Mongols were cruel, and their reign led to an age of intolerance in Islam.

As the Mongols gained control, some of their leaders accepted Islam and led their empire as Muslims. It was a tumultuous period, to be replaced by the Ottoman Empire, which arose in

---

[55] Afshin Marashi, "The Nation's Poet: Ferdowsi and the Iranian National Imagination," in *Iran in the 20th Century: Historiography and Political Culture*, edited by Touraj Atabaki (London: I.B. Tauris, 2009), 110-111.

[56] Richard M. Eaton, "Approaches to the Study of Conversion to Islam in India," in *Religious Movements in South Asia 600-1800*, edited by David N. Lorenzen (Delhi: Oxford University Press, 2004), 111.

Istanbul at the seat of the former Byzantine Empire. It was run by Turks, who had been known as military experts. They had been key in establishing the Fatimid Empire in Egypt, run by former Mamluk slaves, as well as the militaries of the kingdoms in Persia. Ottoman rule would last until the 20th century and would continually adapt as it was pressured more and more by Europe. Not long after the Ottoman Empire was established, the Safavid Empire arose in Persia, which would institute some unique features of its own.

Islam Develops in the East

The Safavids were the first empire to officially claim Shi'i Islam as the official religion, which has still held as the majority religion in present day Iran. The Safavid era also gave birth to many Persian poets with Sufi tendencies, an outworking of the Sufism often identified with Persians. Sufism was a movement seen throughout the Islamic world, but especially in the areas of Iraq and Iran (and eventually India), as people followed a specific teacher whose aim was to help devotees better show love to Allah, and experience Allah's love. The development of Sufism within a Shi'ite culture (which is typically considered more severely exclusive), shows diversity in Islam. It's not the monolithic, coldly orthodox belief system that many people believe.[57] The regional cultural characteristics of Islam can be seen even more as one studies the spread of Islam farther east.

The Mughal Empire was founded in present day Afghanistan and Northern India, initially by a military force led by a man of Mongol and Tamerlane blood. The Mughal Empire had many cultural challenges to overcome given its location in the middle of Hindu India. One of the early sultans, Akbar, was known for his openness to cultural expression, and this reputation drew

---

[57] Heinz Halm, *Shi'ism*, second edition (New York: Columbia University Press, 2004), 49.

many Persian poets and artists to his realm. It was a period of cultural flowering as well as a time of tolerance for the Hindu tendencies of local rulers and an affinity for Sufi teachings.[58] The greatest examples of artistic prowess in the Mughal Empire are the large, architecturally impressive tombs, including the Taj Mahal. Islam had also entered a more agriculturally fertile and densely populated part of the world than had been seen to the west.

Islam continued to spread throughout India as smaller kingdoms gave their allegiance to the larger Mughal empire. In India, Islam spread more as a religion of the plow than as a religion of the sword.[59] It was the means by which people could organize themselves and start to work together as a community sharing experience and expertise in farming. Some Muslims introduced new crops such as rice to India. At the same time, they brought their religion to a people who lacked a structured belief system. Even so, some of the local leaders under this empire were allowed to retain their Hinduism. While most subjects in a kingdom would likely have accepted the new religion of their ruler without protest, there were probably examples of compulsion to Islam through social pressure and threats as well, even if this was not militarily. As with any form of government, there are always political factors at play, and rulers throughout the world probably accepted the rule of Islam and dealt with it in different ways, especially when it confronted areas that had ascribed to other religions for centuries.

In addition to the initial military push, the agricultural impetus, and the drive for more cultural and political organization, there was another factor in the spread of Islam in India—trade. Arabs would pass through to establish trade connections, and then head on to Malacca on the Malay peninsula and to the Spice Islands to the south and east. As trade continued to spread throughout these islands, their small kingdoms, which were looking for

---
[58] Dale, 80.
[59] Eaton, 120.

a religious system to bind them together, went with Islam. It spread as the local king was convinced to accept it peacefully, and then all of his followers would automatically become Muslims. So the faith spread on these islands because it was chosen by the local kings as a way to bring organized religious legitimacy to their rule. As in India, this was a flexible version of Islam which accommodated many of the animistic and ancestor-venerating practices of the islands.[60] While there is no evidence of foreign military expeditions imposing Islam by conquest in Indonesia, it should be noted that once an Indonesian Islamic state was founded, Islam was sometimes spread by warfare—not necessarily from religious zeal, but rather for dynastic, strategic, and economic reasons.[61]

Present day Indonesia continues to be a very diverse place, even though it is majority Islam. It is doubtful that Islam would have been accepted there had it not been so accommodating to local beliefs already in place. The large group of Muslims that still adhered to local religions on Java, but may have nominally accepted Islam, were referred to as *abangan*. But, within the past century Islamic reform has been very successful and on Java it is difficult to find vocal adherents to *abangan* practice.[62] Still, the flexibility that made Islam palatable to the people of Southeast Asia, so far from the Arab world, a leeway that probably played a major role in their conversion, is now slowly being suppressed in the name of "true, orthodox" Islam. It's happening throughout the Islamic world, as also seen in India with the formation of Pakistan and Bangladesh, and in the establishment of the Islamic Republic of Iran in 1979.

It is difficult to find a pattern in the spread of Islam where people converted because of the appeal of intolerance found in

---

[60] Robert W. Hefner, "Where have all the *abangan* gone?," in *The Politics of Religion in Indonesia*, edited by Michel Picard and Remy Madinier (London: Routledge, 2011).

[61] M.C. Ricklefs, *A History of Modern Indonesia since c. 1200*, Fourth Edition (New York: Palgrave Macmillan, 2008), Location 597.

[62] Hefner, *abangan*, 84.

strictly-scriptural Islam along with the constraints of a system of *shariah* law. Early Islam took power when failing empires were growing weak, and provided a system of religious legitimacy strong enough to consolidate rule. After an initial push that relied on military power, the people in the empire usually followed the conversion of their leaders. The leaders then allowed some Arabization of their unique cultures, without giving up what made them unique. Islam was very accommodating initially of ideas and a variety of artistic expressions, and it even looked appealing to Hindu and animistic peoples because it brought organization to the progress they were making in government, agriculture and trade. The large and diverse empire that Islam commanded could not have been totally controlled religiously, especially as Arab leaders were faced with administering larger populations. And Islam's interaction and accommodation of local cultures and traditions throughout the world facilitated conversions. Furthermore, the Sufis' ability to present Islam in an attractive fashion, principally by emphasizing continuity with rather than change in local beliefs and practices, is often identified as one of the major factors accounting for conversion.[63]

This flexibility of Islamic practice helped it spread because people could join an overall system that helped them be a part of something more universal, but they could still be faithful to their cultures and ancestors. The network and community building that Islam facilitated in the past was also something attractive to disconnected societies. But, as time went on, the discrimination and pressures in areas where Islam already had a majority became the main means of conversion. Islam became the primary means through which formerly disconnected societies found a communal identity, and this unity was a powerful force,

---

[63] Azyumardi Azra, "Opposition to Sufism in the East Indies in the Seventeenth and Eighteenth Centuries" in *Islamic Mysticism Contested: Thirteen Centuries of Controversies and Polemics* edited by Frederick de Jong and Bernd Radtke (Leiden: Brill, 1999), 665.

one strong enough to oppose colonialism in the past.[64] While this unity is a strength of Islam, taking it too far may also be detrimental to the aspects of Islam that drew the initial adherents to the faith.

No matter how much the scholars and leaders of Islam throughout the world want all Muslims to adhere to what they consider orthodox belief, it seems unwise to oppose the accommodating nature of Islam that made it such a presence in the world today. There is enough diversity within the faith that broad generalizations and simplistic explanations of Islam are difficult. Hopefully, as people learn more about Islam, they will see that there are many positive, tolerant moments in Islamic history that will help to balance the largely narrow and negative versions of Islam so widely reported in the Western press. Of course, this is not to gainsay the many genuine examples, in history and today, of Muslim intolerance and aggression. Rather, it is to fill out the picture for the sake of fairness.

---

[64] Hefner, *abangan*, 51.

III

THE INFLUENCE OF TRADE
IN THE SPREAD OF ISLAM

The spread of Islam and Islamic government by the sword is well documented. This method was especially common during medieval times, when Muslim forces played a crucial role in extending Islam's religious and political sway east to India, west to Iberia, north to the Balkans, and south to Nubia and Mali. But the spread of Islam to what could be called the periphery, including Indonesia, is much harder to delineate. Though it depended on a variety of factors, economics set the stage.

Trade routes ensured that Indonesia was not isolated from the outside world, and countries such as Portugal, the Netherlands, Yemen, India, Malaysia, and China often exercised strong influence over the archipelago. Timing was crucial. By dominating the spice trade route for centuries, Arab and Indian traders got first crack at religious impact and, subsequently, the sometimes harsh policies of such "Christian" European powers as Portugal and the Netherlands drove them deeper into the arms this other foreign faith, Islam.

Such is the way of unintended consequences, as Westerners clumsily prompted Indonesians to rally around a faith which could bind them together and legitimize the resistant rule of the various island kingdoms. For example, the establishment of Islamic predominance on Buton, off the southeast coast of Sulawesi, was due less to Muslim trade and more to alarm over European pressure.

Sea Routes to the East

Because the monsoon system was orderly and predictable, seafarers were able to negotiate the Indian Ocean with confidence. In this meteorological context, Southeast Asia enjoyed a strategic position as the maritime checkpoint between India and China, and regional markets can be identified from the third century BC, with some regular maritime trade with India in place by the first century BC. This exchange grew rapidly in the first millennium AD with the emergence of intermediate ports-of-trade. [65]

For centuries, this east-west trade was an intra-Asian land affair, though there had been some contact with Europe thanks to Alexander the Great and his forces, who made it all the way to India in the 4th Century BC. (Through the years, Muslims have counted him an Islamic religious figure; he married a woman from that region, and he is known as Iskandar in Islamic-Persian history.) But it took the emergence of Islam, beginning in the 8th century AD, to foster a full exchange of investment and goods between East and West.

Eventually, Muslim presence was strong from the Mediterranean port of Alexandria to the markets of the Mughal dynasty in India, so European traders could take advantage of an Islamic bridge providing a gateway to the Far East. This was not the same as an Islamic bridge to the Islamic Far East, for while

---

[65] Sebastian R. Prange, "Like Banners on the Sea: Muslim Trade Networks and Islamization in Malabar and Maritime Southeast Asia" in *Islamic Connections: Muslim Societies in South and Southeast Asia* edited by R. Michael Feener and Terenjit Sevea (Singapore: Institute of Southeast Asian Studies (ISEAS), 2009), 26-27.

Muslim land forces had made it as far as Mongolia, they didn't gain the same foothold they'd enjoyed in Central and South Asia. The ancient, overland Silk Road continued as a main commercial thoroughfare, but the growth of European interest in the bounty of the east (encouraged in no small measure by the Italian explorer Marco Polo), encouraged fresh development of sea routes from the Arab Peninsula.[66] Consequently, interest in the land route declined, especially as European fascination with spices such as nutmeg grew.

Most prominently, India proved to be an important stop for those trading with the Arabian Peninsula (usually Yemen). On India's west coast, busy ports emerged -- Gujarat in the north and Malabar in the south, which became "a new international commercial hub, as the strategic intermediary between the Middle East and Southeast Asia."[67] Correspondingly, the busiest ports in Southeast Asia were Malacca on the Malay Peninsula and Aceh on the northern tip of Sumatra in Indonesia, with some farther south in Java.

Arabs, who'd been visiting Malabar since pre-Islamic times, had pressed on to Southeast Asia by the seventh century AD, ever in search of spices. Then, under the Abbasid Caliphate in the 8th century, Muslim traders reached Sumatran (Indonesian) ports. By the ninth century, merchants from Basra (Iraq), Siraf (Iran), and Muscat (Oman) were employing Indian ports to reach Southeast Asia. (A ninth-century shipwreck of Arab or Indian origin discovered in Indonesian waters attests to this activity.)[68]

As the 13th century came to a close, shift to full employment of the sea route was hastened by military and political developments bestride the land route. For instance, since the

---

[66] Craig A. Lockard, "The Sea Common to All: Maritime Frontiers, Port Cities, and Chinese Traders in the Southeast Asian Age of Commerce, ca. 1400-1750," *Journal of World History* 21, no. 2 (2010): 220.

[67] Prange, 28-30.

[68] Michael Flecker, "A Ninth-Century AD Arab or Indian Shipwreck in Indonesia: First Evidence for Direct Trade with China," *World Archaeology* 32, no.3 (February 2001): 336.

Mongols conquered Baghdad and the Abbasid caliphate in 1258, and the Crusaders were driven from the Levant with the fall of Acre in 1291, it became less and less feasible for Europeans to trade from Venice on through Palestine and Baghdad to India.

Egypt, under the Mamluk Sultanate (1250-1517), became the new doorway to and from the East, with a trade route running from Alexandria (Egypt) across the Red Sea to Arabian ports such as Aden (Yemen), and then through Cambay (in Gujarat, India, north of Mumbai/Bombay) to Indonesia.[69] (Around the ninth century, Aden had replaced Siraf as the primary port at the western end of the Indian Ocean; it linked traders to Red Sea trade with Jeddah, Aydhab, and Egypt, to the Arabian caravan routes, and to the Swahili coast.) This route is commonly understood to be a crucial element of Islam's spread from Arabia to Indonesia.

The Yemeni connection was particularly salient, for its merchants were generally drawn from the Hadhramaut sector. Today the generally conservative Hadramis boast the world's highest concentration of descendants of Muhammad (who are known as *sayyid*). Because of their large diaspora communities, which settled in the region, they have been the dominant Arab influence in South and Southeast Asia. They were traditionally seen as having special status since they originated from the homeland of Islam. Their influence ranged throughout India, Singapore, Malaysia, and Indonesia, both economically and politically, during colonialism, with trading communities in each major port city serving the spice trade.[70]

The Indian connection also bolstered Muslim influence in Southeast Asia, for shipping out of the sub-continent was mainly in the hands of the fervently Muslim Gujaratis. Much of the existing literature on commercial interaction and cultural transmission between South Asia and Southeast Asia has

---

[69] Robert Pringle, *Understanding Islam in Indonesia: Politics and Diversity* (Honolulu: University of Hawai'i Press, 2010), 24.

[70] Leif Manger, *The Hadrami Diaspora: Community-Building on the Indian Ocean Rim* (New York: Berghahn Books, 2010), 3.

concentrated on the state of Gujarat, as well as on the Coromandel Coast (in southeast India) and Bengal (Bangladesh). And though trading between India and Southeast Asia, particularly from the Malabar Coast, began with those in the Hindu-Buddhist traditions, the Muslim trading networks rose to prominence in subsequent centuries[71] – thus a strong Islamic presence at both ends of the sea trading route (Arabia and Southeast Asia).

Sources from the western end of the Indian Ocean depict a burgeoning spice network, dominated by Muslims and centered on the main cultivation regions of Malabar and Southeast Asia. And so the spice trade continued to expand after the thirteenth century, driven by a nearly insatiable European demand. Fortunately, "a spirit of friendly cooperation prevailed between Jew, Muslim, and Hindu (also Christian, although rarely mentioned)." [72]

Thomas Cahill puts this European passion in colorful terms. Speaking of the "spices, opiates, and silks" available only from Asia, he observes that "no one (who was anyone) could any longer imagine doing without these things . . . " (Imagine if Americans could no longer afford chocolate, salt, or cocaine, or if most of the Wal-Marts closed down.) [73]

With Muslims in control of both ends of the trade route, the importance of Indonesian ports with their Muslim traders and Islamic communities grew. Nevertheless, devotees of other religious groups were substantial players in the region. For instance, a Hindu prince from the Sriwijaya kingdom founded a new port at Malacca, on the Malaysian side of the Straits of Malacca, not long after 1400.

It became successful because it was strong enough to eliminate rather than practice piracy, and well-governed

---

[71] Prange, 25.
[72] Ibid., 30-31.
[73] Thomas Cahill, *Heretics and Heroes: How Renaissance Artists and Reformation Priests Created Our World* (New York: Random House/Anchor, 2013), 41.

enough to offer foreign traders a safe, congenial place to re-provision, exchange goods, and store them. Most important, and the key factor in explaining the need for such a port, traders needed a place to await the seasonal change in monsoonal winds which determined what direction they could go at any given time of year, whether toward China and the Spice Islands or toward India.[74]

Despite beachheads of influence from the cultures to the north, Indonesians still held these outsiders collectively at arm's length. Her islands were populated by many kingdoms, but they maintained a loose sense of common identity.

> The people of coastal Southeast Asia, particularly those touched by Malay culture, identified themselves as "below the winds" in relation to India and all points west, which were "above the winds." Europeans, even when they came across the Pacific as the Spanish did, were quickly understood to be part of that world "above the winds" in which Hinduism, Buddhism, Islam, and such powerful associated symbols as Alexander the Great and the empire of "Rum" [referring to governments and people in lands of the former Eastern Roman Empire] all had their origin.[75]

Islam Gains Traction in Indonesia

From first contact, something on the order of five hundred years passed before Indonesia manifested significant signs of Islamic influence.

---

[74] Pringle, 24-25.
[75] Anthony Reid, "Early Southeast Asian Categorizations of Europeans" in *Implicit Understandings: Observing, Reporting, and Reflecting on the Encounters Between Europeans and Other Peoples in the Early Modern Era* edited by Stuart B. Schwartz (Cambridge: Cambridge University Press, 1994), 268-269.

From the tenth to the mid-twelfth centuries, envoys with Muslim-sounding names traveled to China from Sriwijaya, the great entrepot port on the Straits of Malacca. A tombstone with a Muslim date found in Leran, East Java, dates from 1082. More of this scattered evidence exists, but it has limited meaning. In any case, there were no doubt colonies of Muslim traders in Indonesia's port communities well before any substantial religious change.[76]

It's tempting to see Muslim seafarers as an army of erstwhile proselytizers, and, indeed, the Quran repeatedly refers to maritime trade and even describes the sails of ships as portents of the faith, "like banners on the sea" (42:32). But "historians have been reluctant to see merchant sojourners as sources of cultural transmission," despite the special opportunities expatriate merchants had for cultural brokering.[77] But it cannot be denied that traders opened the way for acquaintance and impact.

Islamization definitely began at the top of society, similar to Hinduization eight centuries previously:

> For the rulers of rich civilizations such as that of the Javanese, Islam seems to have offered no new and desirable features. Islam's major political distinction, the theoretical equality of all believers, probably did not appeal at all to the Indonesian aristocracy. However, Islam was the religion of the booming trade routes, and it brought exciting new political as well as economic opportunities. Muslims held key positions in the officialdoms that ran the ports, and soon gained enough status to possibly marry into ruling families. If intermarriage had required conversion to Islam, it could have been that a threadbare aristocracy would trade status

---

[76] Pringle, 23.
[77] Prange, 35.

for money. In other cases, the rulers themselves received some of the profits of the trade and participated in it, directly or through royal agents. As rulers converted to Islam, and became sultans, and as word spread of powerful new Islamic realms in India and elsewhere, Islam itself gained status. When Europeans entered the region, Islam offered a unifying, international bond of partnership and some degree of protection against these dangerous, well-armed rivals.[78]

The earliest evidence of a ruler's conversion comes in the form of a gravestone, dated 1211 AD, at Lamreh in Aceh. Conversions among the local population also register from the early thirteenth century but appear to have occurred in significant numbers only from the late fourteenth century onwards.[79]

---

[78] Pringle, 29-30.
[79] Ibid., 35-36.

IV

THE PORTUGUESE AND TERNATE

The Hindu prince who founded the Malay port of Malacca, became a Muslim not long before his death in 1414, taking the name Iskandar Shah. His successors developed the port to prominence, attracting Javanese traders who once dealt directly with India, and its prestige also stimulated the spread of Islam throughout the smaller ports in Indonesia, including those on the north coast of Java.[80]

In 1497 the Portuguese explorer Vasco de Gama reached India, and in 1511 Alphonse d'Albuquerque conquered Malacca. "The Portuguese were not strong enough to monopolize the spice trade, as the Dutch later did, so many Muslim traders ceased coming to Malacca, and scattered to other locations, bringing some nearby ports to prominence -- Aceh on north Sumatra, Johor on the tip of the Malay Peninsula, and eventually Demak on Java. By the end of the fifteenth century, Muslim ports were challenging the power of Majapahit [the Hindu-Buddhist empire] and soon had Malacca under siege."[81]

As Islam spread, some rulers might have tried to convert their neighbors by force, but political ambition rather than religion was the normal motive.

---

[80] Ibid., 25-27.
[81] Ibid.

The evidence taken together points to a slow and gradual process: by the end of the thirteenth century Islam was established in north Sumatra; in the fourteenth century in northeast Malaya, Brunei, parts of east Java, and the southern Philippines; in the fifteenth century in Malacca and other areas of the Malay Peninsula; in the sixteenth century the coastal areas of central and east Java were mostly Islamic while its western region and much of the interior were not.[82]

The first Javanese Muslim state, Demak, makes for an interesting case study, both of Muslim accomplishment and Portuguese blunder. Having toppled what was left of the ancient Hindu-Buddhist Majapahit Empire, Demak's new Muslim rulers lacked pedigree, but they had money and ambition, and some of them fought in the name of religion. The Hindu-Buddhist ruler of Banten, a pepper port on the western end of the north coast of Java, saw this happening and asked the Portuguese for an alliance in 1522. The agreement gave the Europeans permission to open a post at nearby Sunda Kelapa, the site of modern Jakarta, but the Portuguese sailed away without acting. When they returned five years later, they found that Muslim Demak had conquered Hindu Banten in the intervening period, and they were not allowed to remain.[83] (The Dutch eventually took control of this port in 1619 and later began to build Batavia, which is now Jakarta.)

The Portuguese were more concerned with the small island of Ternate farther east, in the heart of the Spice Islands, known as the Malukus.

The first Portuguese Captain in Maluku was Francisco Serrao sent there by Albuquerque in 1511. Pigafetta, who

---

[82] Ronit Ricci, *Islam Translated: Literature, Conversion, and the Arabic Cosmopolis of South and Southeast Asia* (Chicago: The University of Chicago Press, 2011), 6.
[83] Pringle, 30.

arrived two years after his death there in 1521, happened to report that he left two children by a woman he had married in Java, presumably during that first voyage from Malacca in 1511. We have to assume that the harshness of the initial Portuguese entrance into Southeast Asia was very quickly modified by relationships such as these.[84]

The Portuguese were received warmly in Ambon and Ternate (both in the Malukus), and their presence was seen as an exceptional windfall because of the commerce they would bring. Some Portuguese chroniclers relate that the Ternate ruler maximized the effect of his new Portuguese allies by claiming they were the fulfillment of a local prophecy: "That the time would come, when Iron Men should arrive at Ternate, from the remotest parts of the world, and settle in its Territory; by whose power the glory and dominion of the Moluco [*sic*] islands should be far extended."[85]

The Portuguese benefitted from a sense of affinity, for the Malukans were always waging war, and enjoying it, and they considered the Portuguese as formidable warriors. As esteemed combatants, they soon became significant players in interstate rivalries among the neighboring kingdoms of the Malukus.[86]

Despite evidence of positive interaction between the locals and the Portuguese, there were several key negative events that contributed to the solidification of Islamic identity among the Indonesians. Since the Christians had just reclaimed control of Spain from Muslim rule during this period, Portugal's aggressive campaign to capture the spice trade could have been seen as an extension of that struggle. The Portuguese, like the Dutch after them, were primarily concerned with profit, not converts.[87] The Portuguese attacked the ships of Muslim traders, often killing

---

[84] Reid, 273.
[85] Ibid., 278-280.
[86] Ibid.
[87] Pringle, 27-28.

Southeast Asian pilgrims on their way to Mecca. This confirmed the earlier idea held by Muslims in the Indian Ocean that these were "Franks," (Malay *Ferringi*), the same people who had attacked the holy places during the Crusades.[88] At one point the rulers of Gujarat and Yemen complained about this practice to the Sultan of Egypt, who sent an envoy to the Pope, who wrote a letter to the King of Portugal, who predictably did nothing.

Later, during the reign of Suleiman the Magnificent, the Acehnese sought and received military assistance from Turkey (probably in about 1540) against the pagan Batak people of the interior, and certainly in 1568, against the Portuguese. Though Indonesian rulers sometimes used the banner of Islam as an ideological weapon, the struggle for the spice trade was primarily a matter of power politics and commercial rivalry.

The Portuguese, who dominated Malacca[89] for more than 100 years after 1530, followed a strictly anti-Islamic policy and did whatever they could to prevent further spread of the Muslim religion. When, in 1641, the Dutch succeeded in defeating the Portuguese, they chose a more tolerant policy of religion and attempted to cooperate with the Islamic Malay sultanates.[90] Unfortunately the Portuguese were the first to arrive and set a religiously antagonistic tone for the future.

Predictably, there was pushback. Both in Calicut and Aceh, the two regions vital to the Muslim spice networks, Muslim traders initially "arose in a spirit of counter-crusade against

---

[88] Reid, 275.

[89] Malacca is a city on the west coast of Peninsular Malaysia, and is also the name given to the strait where the city is found. Maluku (historically also known as the Moluccas) refers to the islands just east of the island of Sulawesi in Indonesia where the islands of Ternate and Ambon are located and are the Spice Islands because they are where cloves and nutmeg originate from. Malacca and Maluku will be referred to several times throughout this book because they each have historical significance, and even though their names sound similar they are very distinct places.

[90] Sven Cederroth, "Indonesia and Malaysia" in *Islam Outside the Arab World* edited by David Westerlund and Ingvar Svanberg (New York: St. Martin's Press, 1999), 265-266.

the Portuguese." Their resistance to the Portuguese monopoly claims is evident from the extensive discussions of so-called "piracy" in the European sources.

All along, there were searches for alternatives. While local Muslim traders had little choice but to confront the Portuguese, the wealthy expatriate merchants were able to relocate and reorganize their activities.[91] Consequently, by the 1530s,

> [A] new Muslim trade route developed from Aceh via the Maldives to the Red Sea, which carried as much pepper to Europe as did the Portuguese on the Cape route. In 1569, the Archbishop of Goa griped that so much pepper was arriving in Mecca from Aceh that some of the surplus was re-exported to Gujarat![92]

So Portuguese attempts to stifle Muslim influence produced more direct contact with the homeland of Islam as strictly Muslim trade networks developed. And while the kingdoms of the Spice Islands (notably Ternate) made the most of their relationship with the Portuguese while it benefitted them, as the antagonism between Muslims and the Portuguese increased, their relationship was strained.

Ternate and Buton

The ruler of Ternate was the first to embrace Islam in the Spice Islands, sometime in the last quarter of the fifteenth century. According to Ternaten traditions, Java was the source and inspiration of the new religion in north Maluku. A Javanese trader named Hussein is credited with introducing the faith to Ternate, while a later Javanese priest from Giri is acknowledged as "the most important propagator of that religion in this region." Nevertheless, around 1536, Islam was still confined principally

---

[91] Prange, 33.
[92] Ibid., 34.

to the ruler, his family, and those of his followers. This situation had not changed radically since Tome Pires's observations two decades earlier that, though the Malukan rulers were Muslim, three-fourths of the people remained unconverted. Over time, though, there was a gradual acceptance of Islam by the people, and Islamic posts were created in the port city, bringing to the faith major economic benefits and prestige. Muslim traders and scholars preferred to go to ports where they were assured a mosque for worship and the protection of a Muslim ruler.[93] The Sultan of Buton to the south (centered on an island smaller than the American state of Delaware) followed suit by accepting Islam in 1540, underscoring the influence Ternate had in the region.

The sixth ruler of Buton, Murhum, was the first king of Buton to accept Islam. (He was given the title of "sultan" by Sheik Abdul al-Wahid). According to the tradition, Islam had been brought to Buton by an Arab from Gujarat named Abdul Wahid, who landed in Burangasi around the year 1527 after stopping in Johor. According to Butonese historian Zahari, his second visit was in 1542, but Dutch historian Pim Schoorl believes it was 1540.[94] It was on this second visit that Buton officially accepted Islam.

Buton had apparently felt economic, political, and military pressure from Ternate and increasingly saw the value of Islam in legitimizing their kingdom. The many islands under the rule of the Sultanate of Buton likely followed as word spread of Islam, and Ternate continued to encourage the process as they exerted their authority in the region and hardened their position against the Portuguese. Thus, Ternate's relationship with the Portuguese

---

[93] Leonard Andaya, *The World of Maluku: Eastern Indonesia in the Early Modern Period* (Honolulu: University of Hawai'i Press, 1993), 57-58.

[94] Tawalinuddin Haris, "Benteng Keraton Buton," in *Monumen: karya persembahan untuk Prof. Dr. R. Soekmono*, edited by Edi Sedyawati and Ingrid H.E. Pojoh (Depok: Fakultas Sastra, Universitas Indonesia, 1990), 325-328.

that started well ended very badly.

The sultans of Ternate were usually chosen for their physical prowess and spiritual potency, but not necessarily their mastery of the teachings of Islam. Sultan Hairun of Ternate (ruled 1535-1570) dressed like a Portuguese, spoke their language fluently, and governed his kingdom with an assurance bred of long familiarity and friendship with Portuguese officials. The Portuguese, and later the Dutch and English, continued to deal almost exclusively with these sultans, assuring them unimpeded access to foreign goods and the ability to preserve the center's prestige.[95] But Hairun became disillusioned with the Portuguese and became known as a "strong defender of the Islamic faith." Given the generally negative reputation of the Portuguese among Muslims, as the people of Maluku became more Islamic and better understood the profit that could be made by controlling a portion of the spice trade, it came time for these Europeans to go.

The Portuguese had experienced Muslim occupation of their Iberian homeland, and had subsequently engaged in a long and bloody North African campaign, where they struggled with the Barbary Pirates. This conditioned them for continued struggle against Islam in Maluku.[96] Sultan Hairun became increasingly irritating to the Portuguese "by his ability to manipulate them to advance his own authority and that of Islam."[97] But even with their military might, they were not in a position to hold Ternate against a unified uprising, which was also the case with other Portuguese holdings throughout the archipelago.

Sultan Hairun's growing opposition to the Portuguese ended with his assassination at their hand in 1570. Power transferred to his son, Sultan Babullah (ruled 1570-1583), who made it his

---

[95] Andaya, 58.
[96] Ibid., 123.
[97] Anthony Reid, "Islamization and Christianization in Southeast Asia: The Critical Phase, 1550-1650," in *Southeast Asia in the Early Modern Era: Trade, Power, and Belief* edited by Anthony Reid (Ithaca: Cornell University Press, 1993), 165.

mission to restore Islam to its "rightful prominence" in Maluku and to expel the Portuguese. Most of the Portuguese and native Christians expelled from Ternate resettled in Ambon, although some of the Portuguese married to local women remained behind. Later the neighboring island kingdom of Tidore opened its lands to the Portuguese, but Ternate would remain staunchly Islamic.[98]

The alliance or control of the nearby kingdom of Buton (or "Butung") vacillated between the more powerful neighboring kingdoms of Gowa (in the current Indonesian city of Makassar, not to be confused with Goa in India) to the west and Ternate to the northeast. After Babullah assumed power in Ternate, he undertook campaigns to the periphery of his kingdom to assert his overlordship.[99] Buton had a consistently high status in Maluku since it enjoyed the shared prestige of having kings who could trace their descent to one of the four mythical sea dragon eggs from which the original kings of Maluku emerged.[100] Then, as Ternate became more Islamic, and the Kingdom of Gowa also accepted Islam in the early seventeenth century, the position of Islam was further solidified in Buton.

In most parts of Indonesia, Islam passed through many hands until it reached the people on the remotest islands. This eastward march of Islam extended far from the Arabian Peninsula and interacted with the cultures of many great civilizations. This interaction changed those cultures in some ways, but Islam itself would also adapt. From Yemen to India to Malaysia to Indonesia, Islam followed trade routes that had been operating for centuries, and which steadily increased in importance as demand for spices increased in Europe. It so happened that the increasingly popular religion of Islam, which helped legitimize rulers in the archipelago, proved also to be a powerful tool to unite these kingdoms against the power of the Portuguese and

---

[98] Andaya, 131-133.
[99] Ibid., 134.
[100] Ibid., 88.

later the Dutch. Even the relatively small island kingdom of Buton had a ruler who determined that his right to rule would be further solidified by accepting Islam before the other kingdoms of Sulawesi. Buton's strategic position gave it a small role in the Islamization of the islands of the spice trade, and so helped shape the Indonesia that we know today.

V

THE INFLUENCE OF SUFISM IN THE SPREAD OF ISLAM

Clearly, spice trade routes to Southeast Asia, which were dominated by Arabs and Indians, were a major factor in the spread of Islam to Indonesia, but this explanation alone is not sufficient. Traders carried other beliefs and religious practices throughout the archipelago, but something made Islam especially attractive to the rulers and people of these island kingdoms. One can be fairly certain that it was not the appeal of Arab culture or the requirement to submit to strict religious dogma that led to mass conversions. The people of the Malay Archipelago were much more concerned with mysticism, spiritual power and the heart, and Islam somehow met those needs.[101] Traders who came to the region for economic reasons were probably not responsible for the dissemination of Islamic teachings, though the transportation networks they created and maintained made this dissemination possible. These teachings must have had enough religious flexibility to adapt to the cultures found in Indonesia and sufficient political viability to convince the local rulers to accept it. There is really only one tradition within Islam

---

[101] Azyumardi Azra, *Islam in the Indonesian World: An Account of Institutional Formation* (Bandung: Mizan Pustaka, 2006), 111.

widespread and diverse enough to meet these needs—Sufism. Through understanding the organization and teachings of Sufi orders, as well as expressions of Folk Islam generally referred to as Popular Sufism, the Islamization of the islands and cultures of Indonesia can be better discerned.

Along with the formal forms of Sufism, this formal segment of Islam is also loosely identified with all forms of mysticism within the faith. Mysticism is found in most all religions and is often understood as a "diffuse expression for a world religion to come to terms with a variety of mentalities, a multiplicity of local forms of faith, and yet maintain the essence of its own identity."[102] A study of this mysticism within Islam must begin in Arabia, with a gradually increasing focus on India and eventually Southeast Asia, where Sufism was a major part of Islam's early acceptance.

The influence of Hellenism during the Abbasid Caliphate in Baghdad, often referred to as Islam's "Golden Age," was one of the early open doors to rational thought through which a tradition (though decentralized and unorganized) continues today. The work of Plato and Aristotle had a significant influence on Islam as seen in the work of Ibn Rushd (Averroes), and medical advancements were made by Persian figures such as Ibn Sina (Avicenna).[103] There was also a "degree of integration between biblical and apocryphal materials in the evolving corpus of Islamic literature that reflected the considerable degree of cultural and ethnic assimilation between Jews, Christians and Arabs, which existed at the outset of Islamic history." Some Islamic scholars were against including these "unreliable materials of foreign origin," but they have always had great appeal to the Muslim masses, just as they do today.[104] The Stories of the Prophets,

---

[102] Clifford Geertz, *Islam Observed: Religious Development in Morocco and Indonesia* (New Haven: Yale University Press, 1968), 48.

[103] Jennifer W. Nourse, "The meaning of *dukun* and allure of Sufi healers: How Persian cosmopolitans transformed Malay-Indonesian history," *Journal of Southeast Asian Studies*, 44(3) (October 2013): 405.

[104] Riddell, *Islam*, 67-68.

many of which are found in the Bible, play an important role in disseminating information in Islam.[105] The importance of rationalism in early Islamic thought is usually associated with the Mu'tazila, who thought that "revelation is to be understood in the light of reason." This reliance on an individual commentator's perceptions, individual intuitions, and deductive reasoning soon lost out to the methodologies of individuals such as Ibn Taymiyya and Ibn Hanbal. These two put more emphasis on using other verses of the Quran, *hadiths*, or the teaching of one's predecessors in interpreting difficult verses of the Quran. Others, such as al-Ash'ari, played a crucial role in reconciling the role of revelation and reason in interpreting the Quran: "He affirmed the overwhelming centrality of the divine revelation, the ultimate yardstick against which reform could be measured, but allocated a significant place to reason."[106] The role of reason within Islam is an issue still debated today, but the fact that it played a role in early Islam opened the door to a variety of movements.

Out of this desire to understand Allah apart from what is specifically laid out in the Quran came the mystic desire for intimacy with Allah, an impulse that is usually referred to as Sufism. Sufism is one of the most influential, but rarely talked about, aspects of Islam today. It is so widespread and prominent in the lives of Muslims throughout the world that it offers significant insight into the humanity and uniqueness of Muslims, aspects with which many in the West and those from Christian traditions can probably identify. Sufis want to connect personally with God.

Though some Islamic scholars claim that there is just one universal interpretation of Islam, it is very difficult to control the minds and practices of individual Muslims throughout the world. Sufism is a response to the cold, impersonal expressions of Islam that are usually associated with Islamism, and the majority of

---
[105] Ibid., 64.
[106] Ibid., 21-23.

Muslims in Asia have Sufi tendencies. It is interesting to note that in Arabia, Sufism arose in response to a more conservative Islam that had already taken root, but in the Malay world, it was just the reverse: Sufism took root initially and dominated for centuries, but more "orthodox" Islam then emerged in response to it.[107]

Among the prominent Sufis in early Islamic history were al-Hallaj (Persian, d. 922), al-Ghazali (Persian, d. 1111), Ibn al-Arabi (Spanish, d. 1240), Jamal al-Din al-Rumi (Persian, d. 1273), and Hafiz (Persian poet, d. 1389/90). Today, Sufism is found throughout the Muslim world, and it finds its source in early Islam. Al-Hallaj was a Sufi involved in the spread of Islam to Gujarat, India, and from there it went to Indonesia. Ibn al-Arabi was looked to by the Malay for inspiration.[108] These prominent Sufi thinkers are generally accepted throughout the Muslim world, but Sufism has traditionally been marked by following the teachings of a specific saint (*pir* or *shaykh*). The teachings of this specific individual are usually said to trace back to the teachings of Muhammad, and while they are often marked with an identifiable stream of thought, the complete body of teachings is not available to the general public. Sometimes meaningful distinctions between brotherhoods were blurred, and membership in a brotherhood signified little more than an additional title to one's name. When the *shaykh* himself belonged to two brotherhoods simultaneously, his followers identified with neither one in particular, but rather with the person of the *shaykh*.[109]

---

[107] Ibid., 322.
[108] Ibid., 71-72.
[109] Nehemia Levtzion, "Eighteenth Century Sufi Brotherhoods: Structural, Organizational and Ritual Changes" in *Islam: Essays on Scripture, Thought and Society: A Festschrift in Honour of Anthony H. Johns* edited by Peter G. Riddell and Tony Street (Leiden: Brill, 1997), 153.

Persia

Persia (Iran) played a very important role in early Islam. Persia was the first culture (other than Arabic) to assume Islam, and the reach of this empire was far enough that it played a role in the development of Islam in India. Persia had been Arabized to a certain extent with the entrance of Islam, but the opulent and eccentric environment of the court culture in the former Persian empire can be seen in stories such as those of Scheherazade in the Arabian nights. The court culture was very influential in the Abbasid Empire, which provided an environment for Persian art and thought to flourish. This was not a rigid society based on *shariah* law, but that of a king who made decisions in accordance with his desires and judgments, in ways similar to those of other kingdoms in medieval times. Many of these early Islamic Empires appropriated, and added to, the cultures they were based upon and showed the highest form of cultural sophistication and thought for their day. Islam generally appropriated cultural traditions rather than constructed them. In the past Islam encouraged and promoted cultural beauty in areas it governed instead of destroying this creativity in the name of religion, an approach not typically the case in more recent history.[110]

A look at Islam's development in Central and South Asia provides helpful background for understanding its development in Indonesia. After the Mongols arrived and destroyed the center of the Abbasid Caliphate in Baghdad, several Islamic empires eventually emerged and Islam became even more diverse and widespread. The Safavid Empire arose in Persia and adopted the Shi'ism that is the majority in Iran today. Turkic peoples migrated in large numbers to the Anatolian Peninsula and established the Ottoman Empire on the ruins of the former Byzantine Empire. Islam also moved by land eastward past

---

[110] Shahab Ahmed, *What is Islam? The Importance of Being Islamic* (Princeton: Princeton University Press, 2016. Kindle Electronic Edition).

the heart of Persia, through the area around Afghanistan, where tradition has it that the messianic figure of Islam, the Mahdi, will emerge along with a military force heralding the end of the world.[111] But the greatest Islamic empire in the region was a little farther to the east.

India

The Mughal empire in India was the most significant and powerful in the region, and was founded by Babur, whose father was a descendent of Tamerlane and whose mother was a descendent of Ghengis Khan. (The word "Mughal" is Persian for "Mongol.")[112] Prior to the rise of the Mughal empire there were several smaller dynasties on the Indian subcontinent, which have been labeled the "Delhi sultans," many of which were ethnically Turk, and in some cases descended from military slaves. There was significant Persian influence on these sultanates, and they were generally tolerant of the large number of Hindu rajas who were allowed to rule as tributary vassals as long as they paid tax as *dhimmis*.[113] That is to say, in these medieval Islamic empires, subjects with a faith different from Islam were not always forced to convert, but were pressured to conform through discrimination and taxes associated with being a *dhimmi*.[114] The arts also played a significant part of the Ottoman, Safavid, and Mughal empires. While the Ottomans and Safavids built some significant mosques and *madrasas*, the Mughals are best known for their tombs, despite the fact that some *hadiths* denounce elaborate funerary monuments as non-Islamic. Again, this is a clear indicator of the increasing influence

---

[111] Jean-Pierre Filiu, *Apocalypse in Islam* (Berkeley: University of California Press, 2011), 28-29.
[112] Stephen F. Dale, *The Muslim Empires of the Ottomans, Safavids, and Mughals* (New York: Cambridge University Press, 2010), 17.
[113] Ibid., 22-26.
[114] Mark Durie, *The Third Choice: Islam, Dhimmitude, and Freedom* (Deror Books, 2010).

of Sufism.¹¹⁵ The Timurid culture (descendants of Tamerlane) was also well-known for its painting style, poetry, and elaborate gardens during this time period. The poetry of Persia and India usually dealt with subjects such as love, which is another trait of Sufism. Over time, rulers spent too much time seeking their own pleasure, and this situation combined with other regional factors to precipitate the eventual collapse of the Mughal Empire in the 18th century. Thus, Indian Muslims were no longer part of an Islamic empire and were living in a Hindu majority nation. This led to the eventual creation of Pakistan as a state for Muslims, and then by the creation of Bangladesh when the state of East Pakistan declared independence.¹¹⁶

The usual accounts on how large numbers of South Asians converted to Islam point to "the sword," to political pressure, or to a search for relief from the caste system, but, for one thing, the regions that are most Islamic were not those that received the most political pressure from Islamic leaders. Rather, they were converted through peaceful means. Eaton proposes that a process of accretion and reform is a helpful way to explain this phenomenon, for slow growth and accumulation were the primary means of Islam's entry, with several periods of reform to keep things on track.¹¹⁷ Accretion would probably retain the original cosmology, while reform would:

> "distinguish the Islamic supernatural agencies from the pre-existing cosmological structure and repudiate the local beliefs. Another way to distinguish between accretion and reform is by studying the overall socio-political environment. The early phase of mass conversion generally accompanied integration into the outer fringes of one of the expanding Indo-Muslim states in a regional

---
¹¹⁵ Dale, 148.
¹¹⁶ Ibid., 290.
¹¹⁷ Eaton, 111.

context. In that whatever Muslim elements were added onto the existing stock of beliefs and practices were not perceived as representing a 'world' religion, but only the particular beliefs and practices associated with a local saint (*pir* or *shaykh*), a local *qadi* (Muslim judge) or the spiritual power of a local shrine. On the other hand, the context of reform was a worldwide one, inspired by a vision of Islam as a world religion, with Mecca as its geo-spiritual hub."[118]

The ebb and flow of this process of accretion and reform led to the state of Islam we see in South Asia today, one similar to what we find in Malaysia and Indonesia.

The regions more susceptible to mass conversion would be those that had not yet integrated a written tradition into their society. Islam would fill that void by stabilizing religious patterns with just such a thing. Another factor would be that the social and ecological situation of frontier and fringe areas would be more open than the heartland cultural regions to *qadis* and Sufi shrine influence. On the fringes were "non-agrarian forest or pastoral peoples that had not yet been indoctrinated into Hindu agrarian society." So as agrarian infrastructure was developed and the state expanded religiously and politically, these indigenous, non-Hindu, non-agriculturalists were gradually transformed into Muslim agriculturalists. This led Eaton to observe that "Islam seems to be more of a religion of the plough than a religion of the sword in India."[119]

Another recurring characteristic in the Mughal empire was its tolerance of other faiths, especially that of the Hindus living under its sway. The sultan most well-known for his tolerance was Akbar, who also oversaw the rise of the Mughal Empire to its early glorious years. His ruling principle of "peace with all" has gained him charismatic status among Indian and Western

---
[118] Ibid., 111-113.
[119] Ibid., 118-120.

intellectuals today.[120] It is also notable that around the year 1600, the Mughal empire ruled over an empire incorporating as many as 145 million subjects in a relatively fertile area known for agriculture and trade, compared to 22 million in the Ottoman empire (Turkey) and ten million under the Safavids (Persia), both having less fertile land.[121] Trade was continually a major source of income for the Mughal Empire, while changes in the major trade routes of the European powers caused serious problems for the Ottoman Empire in the 17th century.[122] These maritime trade routes passed through India, and provided a channel for Sufi thought and practice to spread.

Certain aspects of Sufism are recognizable throughout the world today, the most prevalent being the veneration of gravesites. It's seen throughout Indonesia as well as in India, where the great architectural achievements of the Mughal Empire were in the construction of tombs. Buildings such as the Taj Mahal are Muslim tombs, specifically Sufi.

---

[120] Dale, 80.
[121] Ibid., 107-108.
[122] Ibid., 133.

VI

ORTHODOX AND POPULAR SUFISM

There are many aspects of popular Sufism that are dismissed as heretical, but orthodox Sufism is not guilty of this charge. The great Muslim theologian, al-Ghazali, played an important role in making Sufism orthodox because he said that following *shariah* was also important. He argued that in order to follow *shariah* well, it is important to get one's heart right with Allah first.[123] So Sufism oscillated between individualist renunciation of this world and community-oriented, legalist world-affirmation.[124]

Al-Ghazali is seen by many as the most important figure in the reconciliation of Sufism and normative Islam. He has been criticized by some for separating inner (*dhahir*) and outer (*batin*) aspects of worship, but for many he is seen as wedding them together.[125] For example, his writing encourages mandatory ritual Islamic prayer (*salat*), but noted that "Two members of my Community may perform the Prayer in such a way that their bowing and their prostration are as one, yet their Prayers may be

---

[123] Ibid., 74.
[124] Levtzion, 154.
[125] Khurram Murad, "Foreword," in al-Ghazali, 8-9.

as far apart as heaven and earth (in respect to their humility)."[126] Normative Sufism has always been about adherence to Islamic law and a heart right with God.

The Breadth of Sufism

The challenge that Sufism has always faced, and continues to face today, is the broad sweep of practices that fall within the category of Sufi. In the 11th century a theme emerged in Sufi writings that "true Sufism" had disappeared and there were no real Sufis left anymore. Original Sufism was not about formal practice, but about morals. Even so, over time opinions began to emerge about the way Sufis were supposed to act and dress. There were also Sufi masters emerging that held a high status, claiming to have assumed the mantle of earlier Sufi masters while leading many followers with unquestioning authority. Hujwiri (d. between 1073-1077), the author of the first major survey of Sufism in Persian, discussed Sufi approaches by organizing them into different groupings, illustrated by this list: 'states and stations' (under Muhasibi), 'intoxication and sobriety' (under Bayazid and Junayd), 'altruism' (under Nuri), 'lower soul and passion' (under Tustari), 'friendship with God and miracles' (under Tirmidhi), 'subsistence and passing away' (under Kharraz), 'union and separation' (under Sayyari) and 'the nature of the human spirit' (under Hallaj).[127] Sufism began to organize itself into different paths in which the teachings of an ancient Sufi master were passed down in a type of spiritual genealogy.

Pedigrees and spiritual lineages of Sufi masters (*shaykh*) seemed to say one's whole Sufi outlook is authenticated by pedigree. One's *shaykh* was vitally important and purported to

---

[126] al-Ghazali, *Inner Dimensions of Islamic Worship*, trans. from the *Ihya' 'Ulum al-Din* by Muhtar Holland (Leicestershire: The Islamic Foundation, 1983), 23.
[127] Karamustafa, 100-102.

be almost as crucial as Muhammad in the life of his follower (*murid*). A story in the Quran (Kahf 18: 60-82) was used as an illustration of the importance and difficulty of following a *shaykh* without question. An unnamed servant of God appeared to Moses in this passage, and Moses asked to follow him in order to obtain his special knowledge (*ilm*). The man agrees as long as Moses promises to never question anything that he does. Moses cannot keep his promise after the man does some outrageous acts, so the relationship is terminated. The implications of this story used by a *shaykh* was that he had a special knowledge even Moses was denied, and it was important to follow him without question.[128] The unquestionable authority of the *shaykh* created a lack of accountability in which outrageous behavior and heretical teachings sometimes arose, which led to the tarnishing of the reputation of Sufism.

In the earlier years there were Sufis who sacrificed everything for God, but more and more over the years there were those that lived in lodges (*ribat*) and used "Sufism" for their own profit and displayed the greed they had for the things of this world. The excesses of some Sufi *shaykh*, as well as the tendency of some of them to lean towards antinomianism, led al-Ghazali to write a treatise against these "Sufi pretenders."[129] Despite efforts such as these by Sufi scholars, the increasing popularity of Sufism in the 12th century and its confluence with popular sainthood and popular religiosity led to its generally negative reputation within normative Islam today, even though the core of Sufism is orthodox. Sufis have also been criticized for delineating between *sharia*, the legal side of Islam, and *haqiqa*, the moral side of Islam, but in reality there should be a balance of both. The Sufi masters of old considered the heart to be of utmost importance when obeying the law of God, and only then could one experience true closeness with their Creator and be called a "friend of God."

---

[128] Ibid., 116-119.
[129] Ibid., 160-166.

Sufism also broadened to include indigenous mystical trends. While early sects such as the "Path of Blame" are an example, the most prominent example today and throughout history are the practices of saint cults. Saint cults were in full bloom by the 11th century. Sainthood and saintly miracles were generally accepted by Islamic scholars, as well as visiting graves to pray and remember, but not visits associated with intercession for the dead and the building of lavish tombs (like the Taj Mahal). People would follow guidelines in conducting rituals at gravesites called *ziyarat*, in order to receive some of the "fluid force that emanated from the saint known as *barakah*. This force permeated the places, persons and objects around him, alive or dead, and its ultimate proof was the saintly miracle, *karama* (or *keramat)*." This grave veneration of saints developed independently from the Sufi concept of sainthood, with a variety of graves receiving this status: graves of the family of Muhammad and his descendants, the Companions and Followers, martyrs of early battles and conquests, Shi'i imams, the first four caliphs, Sufis, "substitutes," rulers, scholars, theologians, and judges.[130] In actuality many of the ritual places some now identify with Sufism actually have little or no direct connection with Islam, such as the graves of rulers, and some are not even graves, but monuments or places that saintly figures visited.[131]

Even though Sufi scholarship and the relationship with the *ulama* was good, "the spread of Sufism among urban and rural masses no doubt only came about as a direct consequence of the increasing conjunction of Sufi sainthood with popular cults of saints during the 11th and 12th centuries."[132] As Sufism gained this greater following there were other consequences. Since some followers of Sufi masters were more serious than others, there arose different categories of devotion instead of everyone

---

[130] Ibid., 130-134.
[131] John Renard, *Friends of God: Islamic Images of Piety, Commitment, and Servanthood* (Berkeley: University of California Press, 2008), 207.
[132] Karamustafa, 143.

following with unquestioning submission. By the end of the 12th century political rulers boosted their legitimacy by seeking the blessing of a Sufi saint. On the other hand, if political rulers felt threatened by a Sufi leader's popularity, they would do away with them if possible.[133] Marshall Hodgson in *The Venture of Islam* says the "human outreach in Sufi masters predicated on a generally tolerant attitude towards diversity and a comprehensive humanity, gave the Sufi tradition a decisive advantage over other forms of religiosity within the Abode of Islam and when combined with the institutional forms which it took constituted an ideal vehicle for a ranging public outreach." The keystone of the whole system was the master-disciple relationship and it was the Sufi master who constituted the center of gravity around which *tariqa*-based Sufism was organized. A Sufi *shaykh* and organizations could reach out to the masses to bring a whole new audience within the Sufi fold, finding in the Sufi *pir (shaykh* in South Asia), especially after his death, both an intercessor and source of blessing.[134]

Orthodox Sufi Brotherhoods and Asia

Sufism is generally disparaged as an unorthodox, backwoods expression of Islam, but it is actually more complicated than that. Many Sufis would say that Muhammad was the first Sufi because, when he received the revelation of the Quran, he went into a trance allowing him to have a special connection with Allah. The example of Muhammad and his closeness to God has been a concern of Sufism since its formative years, with some even claiming that he was a "Perfect Man" who should be emulated.[135] The earliest expressions of Sufism reflected

---
[133] Ibid., 152-155.
[134] Ohlander, Erik S. *Sufism in an Age of Transition: Umar al-Suhrawardi and the Rise of the Islamic Mystical Brotherhoods.* (Leiden: Brill, 2008), 4-5.
[135] Reynold A. Nicholson, *Studies in Islamic Mysticism* (Cambridge: Cambridge University Press, 1921), 78.

an asceticism and mysticism similar to that seen in Christian monasteries, but the emphasis soon shifted from ascetic practice to ecstatic experience.[136]

Some Sufis try to enter into a trancelike state in order to connect with Allah, but as long as the Sufi tradition adheres to an orthodox understanding of Islamic law, or *shariah*, the more mystical side of their belief is tolerable. It has even been argued that Sufi teachings were one of the primary instruments used to align Indonesian Islam to orthodox standards in its early years.[137]

In his book on Islam in South and Southeast Asia, Ricci notes, "The networks of travel, trade, and Sufi brotherhoods, and literary networks were the paths by which Islam spread and flourished."[138] He goes on:

> "The school of Islamic law followed by Javanese and South Indian Muslims living along the coast was one and the same (Shafi'i); contacts in the sphere of Islamic education appear to have been strong, with similar institutions emerging in Tamil Nadu, Sumatra, and Java; Indonesian pilgrims on their way to Arabia used to stop in the Maldives, and in the eighteenth century a Coromandel mosque existed in Batavia (Jakarta). Some of these contacts even increased as colonial powers exiled Indonesians to other countries."[139]

In addition to the influence passed down through Sufi brotherhoods and literary works, Nourse adds that the 'cosmopolitan' Persians also influenced the language and culture of the elite in Indonesia. This happened in a more informal manner, but the role of these mystical healers called *"dukun"* are still found throughout Indonesia, and is one more example

---

[136] Riddell, *Islam*, 69-70.
[137] Laffan, *Islam*, 65.
[138] Ricci, 1.
[139] Ibid., 9.

of how a practice currently seen as very localized among these islands may have had origins in Persia.[140]

The northwest corner of Indonesia is where this outside Muslim contact first began to effect change. A significant place in Indonesian history is the northern tip of the island of Sumatra. Here was the ancient port of Pasai, as well as the Kingdom of Aceh, the point at which Islam first entered the islands we now call Indonesia. Aceh was the first place in the archipelago to become a sultanate, and, through written records, they made a great contribution to our understanding of Islam in the early years. From the very beginnings of Islam in Indonesia one can see that Sufism played a crucial role. In Aceh, a Muslim teacher who came from Gujarat (India) between 1580-1583 saw that the people were not interested in *fiqh* (Islamic jurisprudence) and rhetoric, but they demanded that he teach them *tasawuf* (mysticism) and *kalam* (reason).[141]

Alongside the more formal, sometimes orthodox orders of Sufism, is what is known as Popular Sufism or Folk Islam, which usually shows Sufi tendencies.[142] At a popular level the tendency has been to represent the conversion of rulers to the hitherto unknown faith of Islam as prompted by a supernatural event, driven by the activities of Sufi orders and individual holy men. In this way, Sufism and its mystical traditions facilitated the incorporation of existing South Indian and Southeast Asian customs into the new faith.[143] It is often difficult to differentiate

---

[140] Nourse, 400-422.

[141] Azyumardi Azra, "Opposition to Sufism in the East Indies in the Seventeenth and Eighteenth Centuries" in *Islamic Mysticism Contested: Thirteen Centuries of Controversies and Polemics* edited by Frederick de Jong and Bernd Radtke (Leiden: Brill, 1999), 666.

[142] Riddell, *Islam*, 79.

[143] Sebastian R. Prange, *Like Banners on the Sea: Muslim Trade Networks and Islamization in Malabar and Maritime Southeast Asia* in *Islamic Connections: Muslim Societies in South and Southeast Asia* edited by R. Michael Feener and Terenjit Sevea (Singapore: Institute of Southeast Asian Studies (ISEAS), 2009), 36-37.

the line between local pre-Islamic beliefs and those associated with mystical Islam from other parts of the world. This type of syncretism assuredly takes place, but whether it is an authentic part of the Islamic faith is open for debate since there are so many sources of legitimate authority within the traditions of Islam.

While Popular Sufism, or Folk Islam, was adept at incorporating mystic elements of Islam into pre-existing beliefs, the more formal Sufi orders disseminated the teachings of Sufi theologians into Southeast Asia. Ibn al-Arabi (d.1240) and Abd al-Karim al-Jili (d.1410) developed the concept of "The Perfect Man," which referred to Muhammad, and led to his veneration as bordering on the divine.[144] Al-Hallaj played an important role in the spread of Sufism and Islam to Gujarat, India, and his "Unity of Witness" concept eventually led to the development of the "Unity of Being" concept, that is usually identified with monism (similar to pantheism).

---

[144] Riddell, *Islam*, 75.

VII

THE SEVEN LEVELS (*MARTABAT TUJUH*)

There were seven levels of being (*martabat tujuh*) which individuals would reach on their quest with Allah. And many Sufi orders had secret teachings that would be revealed at the appropriate time by their Sufi master (*shaykh*), who often received his teaching from someone seen as holding the mantle of leadership for an order reaching back to Muhammad.[145] Many attribute the origin of these grades of being to Ibn al-Arabi, who was influenced by Plotinus, and who was a well-known medieval scholar in Muslim Spain (Andalusia). His most influential work traced the unique roles and particular attributes of all the Prophets within Islam, which laid the basis for his teachings on the grades of being.[146] His works also dealt with the subject of religious diversity, which is very timely for Muslims today.[147] His teachings on the grades of being initially identified five grades, but after an Indian scholar published a work where two more grades were added to better describe the

---

[145] Ibid., 35.
[146] Ibn al-Arabi, *The Ringstones of Wisdom (Fusus al-hikam)*, trans. Caner K. Dagli (Chicago: Great Books of the Islamic World, 2004).
[147] William C. Chittick, *Imaginal Worlds: Ibn al-Arabi and the Problem of Religious Diversity* (Albany: State University of New York Press, 1994).

complexity of Allah's Oneness, the teachings on seven grades entered Indonesia and spread throughout the islands.

Hamzah Fansuri was the first documented Malay scholar going to Arabia, where he was initiated into the Qadiriyya Sufi Order, and is known for his teaching on the five grades of being.[148] Another influential scholar in the Malay world was Shams al-Din, who was an early part of the Naqshbandiyya Sufi Order, and who further developed the grades-of-being concept to include seven (*martabat tujuh*). A comparative study of Hamzah's and Shams al-Din's writings points to a shift in influence upon Acehnese mystical thinking from Arab writers (Ibn al-Arabi and al-Jili upon Hamzah) to Indian writers (al-Burhanpuri upon Shams al-Din). "The commentary of Shams al-Din, who based himself on Hamzah Fansuri, both ultimately drew their teachings from famous Arab Sufis such as Ibn al-Arabi and al-Jili. Hamzah and Shams al-Din should be seen primarily as transmitters, rather than innovators. They took Sufi teachings circulating in the Arab world and India and cast them in a Malay mold for the benefit of Malay Muslims."[149]

There are usually seven stages that one must pass through when joining a Sufi order (see table on following page). The first stage is repentance, the key to becoming a Sufi. It is at this point that one attaches himself to a Sufi scholar. From there on follow such stages such as poverty, patience, and mortification of the flesh. Simultaneously, the adherent will reach different states of being, which are not under the control of the teacher, but occur through the grace of Allah. These states are marked by such phenomena as meditation, love, fear, hope, contemplation, and certainty, all in the interest of grasping true reality. Hamzah Fansuri (d. 1590), from Sumatra, considered the stages on the path of mystical knowledge to be *shariah* (the outward prescriptions of the law), *tariqa* (learning from a Sufi master), *haqiqa* (a love-relationship between a Sufi seeker and God), and

---

[148] Riddell, *Islam*, 104.
[149] Ibid., 111-115.

sirr (the secret mystery of God's essence). The ultimate goal is *dhikr* (remembrance) of the innermost being, where the person enters a trance-like state. *Dhikr* is the last stage of *sirr*, and is usually the point at which accusations of heresy could arise. Another characteristic of Sufism is that it is more open to female participation.

Level	Sufi Levels of Being	Arabic Term
1.	Led by the Flesh, Jealous, Hypocrite	*Amarah*
2.	In Control of Yourself	*Lawamah*
3.	Obedient to Your Teacher	*Malhamah*
4.	Peaceful Soul	*Muthma'innah*
5.	Blessing Attained	*Raadliah*
6.	Eternal Blessing	*Mardliah*
7.	Perfection	*Kamaliah*

The number seven also refers to seven different realms in the world (see table on following page), and even has multiple meanings within this concept of realms. These realms not only describe the different realms of reality in the world (including the Oneness of Allah), but also help explain the process through which a spirit is assigned to a developing fetus in a mother's womb. These levels in reverse can also help describe a body as it is decomposing, and the spirit is preparing to leave the corpse.[150] Individuals who master themselves and achieve the seventh level of being can also learn to move freely between some of the different realms of being. For example, if a prophet or someone close to God is in the seventh level, they can connect the Spirit world (level 4) with the Physical World (level 6) through their Imagination (level 5) and what they imagine in their mind happens in the physical world. This allows them to

---

[150] J. W. (Pim) Schoorl, *Masyarakat, Sejarah, dan Budaya Buton* (Jakarta: Penerbit Djambatan bekerjasama dengan Perwakilan KITLV-Jakarta, 2003), 175-177.

do things like fly and transport themselves, as it is believed that Muhammad did in his visit to Jerusalem and when Jesus ascended into heaven. There are also stories throughout the Muslim world about how those close to Allah were able to achieve similar feats. This may also be the way that some individuals are believed to be able to control the weather. The first three levels cannot be fully explained, because they deal with the Oneness of Allah, but in the pantheistic and monistic strains of Sufism the ability for seventh level individuals to enter these realms may be how they explain their ability to achieve extreme closeness to Allah. There could be different versions of these seven levels, and there are certainly different opinions about them, but these tables are provided so the reader can have an introductory understanding of the layers of meaning in the term *martabat tujuh*.

Level	Sufi Realms of Being	Arabic Term
1.	Oneness (of Allah)	*Ahadiyya*
2.	Unity (of Allah)	*Wahda*
3.	Unity in Diversity (of Allah)	*Wahidiyya*
4.	World of Ancestors and People Far Away (Spirits)	*Arwah*
5.	Imagination, Connects Bodies and Spirits (Ideas)	*Mitsal*
6.	The Physical World (Bodies)	*Ajsam*
7.	Can Make Dreams Reality While Awake (Perfect Man)	*Insan*

It has been suggested that if Sufism is like a tree, then the different orders are like the leaves.[151] Indeed, there is not one standard code of doctrine for Sufi practice, but, rather, there are major "orders" or "brotherhoods" (*tariqa* or *tarekat*) based on sets of teachings that originate from an individual with blood

---

[151] Ibid., 76-78, 107-108.

ties to Muhammad. These brotherhoods are the frameworks of orthodox Sufism, calling for obedience to Islamic law along with their mystical pursuits. Some are more widely respected and accepted than others.

Sufism and the Elite

The teachings of these orders do not arise from local beliefs, but are passed down through generations. They were fairly well organized, and "while the colonial powers were entrenching themselves in the Malay world, a plethora of Sufi orders were also penetrating the region and consolidating their presence. The principle orders in this regard were the Qadiriyya, Chishtiyya, Shadhiliyya, Rifa'iyya, Naqshbandiyya, Shattariyya and the Ahmadiyya." The Alawiyya order was also brought to the Malay world by immigrants from the Hadhramaut and played an important role in the spread of Islam in the region.[152]

The *shaykh* of each order are considered to hold special authority, and there is usually a genealogy showing how the mantle of the teaching of the order has been passed down, to ensure faithfulness throughout succeeding generations. Even regular adherents of the order are expected to undergo specialized training in order to guarantee that they understand the teachings correctly, for these mystical teachings are usually complicated. Accordingly, it was often argued that they were not for the common people, but only for the elite, such as the sultans and the ruling establishment. On this model, Sufism was for the elite, and *shariah* was for the masses. For instance, in 1731 on Java, a teacher was tried legally for revealing mystical Sufi truths to the uninitiated,[153] for there was real peril if this knowledge fell into the wrong hands.

Even though the deepest truths may have been for the elite, it was, and still is, a common conviction in the Muslim world that

---
[152] Ibid., 169-170.
[153] Ibid., 23-24.

"Islam is incomplete without attention to the inner dimension."[154] Not surprisingly, though it was often the case that elitist discourse would take place in the classical languages of Arabic and Persian, while Islamic mystical writings were translated into vernacular languages.[155] And though Sufis received much criticism and persecution, many Islamic scholars respected them and noticed that their way of life was often better than that of others.[156] But when it came to leadership of the orders, Sufi pedigrees were powerful and Sufi philosophy was the purview of scholars and sultans, who monopolized the esoteria of the *tarekat*.[157]

Literature also had a role to play in the Islamization of Indonesia. Languages such as Wolio (in Buton) and Javanese had been "Arabacized by the contact with speakers and writers of Arabic and Islamic sources, and we may also think of how Arabic itself, in such a setting, was vernacularized. The spelling, pronunciation, and often also the meaning of Arabic words changed markedly when adopted into Javanese, and Arabic literary genres and themes also took on a local twist." Many of these works were on Sufi topics: "In the early stages of Islamization and contact with Arabic it is likely that Arabic was incorporated for strictly religious purposes into Malay and Javanese. A point was later reached when much of the influx of Arabic was assimilated to a degree that made it 'invisible,' no longer employed for specifically Islamic expression, or at least not exclusively in that context."[158] There were several prominent scholars in the early history of Southeast Asian Islam who were usually associated with a sultanate on Sumatra or the Malay Peninsula, and they left their mark on history through their written works.

One of the primary means of understanding Islam as it developed in Indonesia was through the availability of Arabic

---
[154] Ibid., 35.
[155] Levtzion, 160.
[156] Laffan, *Islam*, 48.
[157] Ibid., 158.
[158] Ricci, 17-19.

commentaries on the Quran translated into Malay. The commentary by al-Baghawi (d.1122) was very popular among the Malay.[159] Another, the commentary by al-Khazin (d.1340), though not well received in Arabia, was very popular in Indonesia because of its narrative style full of miraculous and mystical stories, including those speaking of a just and fair king. Yet another, Al-Baydawi's commentary, was also "held in high regard by early Southeast Asian and Arab Islamic scholars, and still is today, with its concise exegetical comment drawing on a range of approaches."[160] These three commentaries were found to have had sufficient prestige in the Kingdom of Aceh in 1600, then the foremost power among the Malay states, and were considered worthy as a source of instruction in Quranic exegesis for Malay Muslims.[161]

Critics of Sufism

Even though these scholars drew on Sufi teachings from Arabia, they were still severely criticized by some, notably by al-Raniri. Al-Raniri considered the teachings of Hamzah Fansuri and Shams al-Din to be heretical, and with the death of the Sultan Iskandar Muda of Aceh (d.1636) who acted as their patron, al-Raniri came to prominence. The new sultan, Iskandar Thani, appointed al-Raniri as his foremost Islamic scholar. Al-Raniri was born into a mixed Indian and diaspora Hadrami family in Gujarat, India, and received training in Islamic mysticism from the Aydarusiyya Sufi order, but eventually joined the Rifa'iyya. He may have also studied Malay in Gujarat because there was a significant Malay community there. He was most concerned with attacking the "heretical" Wujudiyya (identified with Hamzah and Shams al-Din), who "equated the Creator with the created" and claimed that their state of "involuntary intoxication frees them from their obligations to the behavioral norms of

---

[159] Riddell, *Islam*, 41-45.
[160] Ibid., 141-144.
[161] Ibid., 152.

Islamic law."[162]

This is interesting in light of the fact that the very Rifa'iyya order that al-Raniri identified with is usually known for emphasizing wonders and extreme behavior. One ritual, called *dabbus*, involves the piercing of various parts of the body with no permanent signs of damage. Members of this order have been called "howling dervishes" as a result of certain ritual practices.[163] Even so, al-Raniri brought his concerns before the Sultan and "accused his opponents of effectively claiming divinity for themselves in asserting that they had attained union with God." The Sultan was eventually convinced and issued a *fatwa* that condemned the followers of Shams al-Din to death. Some renounced their previous doctrines to return to orthodoxy, while others did not and were executed.[164] There was also widespread destruction of Shams al-Din's written works.

Something similar happened in the Mughal Empire in the 17th century with the reign of Jahangir. Sufis that had held sway in the Mughal court at the end of the 16th century were then declared heretics by the incoming sultan, even though he was also a Sufi. One of the early Sufis of Arabia, al-Hallaj, was also executed for heresy in 922. In neither case was the issue Sufism, because usually the one ordering the execution was also Sufi. The problem came when individuals claimed they could experience unity with Allah, which not only violated the Oneness of Allah, but it put them in a position of being closer to Allah than the sultan, which had dire consequences.[165] The reason that pantheistic Sufism beliefs were allowed to flourish by some sultans may have been because they reinforced "the popular perception of kingship as one sanctioned, blessed and in-dwelt by Allah."[166] This accorded with the early notion that

---

[162] Ibid., 116-121.
[163] John Renard, *Historical Dictionary of Sufism* (Lanham, Maryland: The Scarecrow Press, Inc., 2005), 202.
[164] Riddell, *Islam*, 123.
[165] Ibid., 124.
[166] Ibid., 112.

Sufism was for the elite, especially the sultan, and was a means to claim special status above the masses.

There arose one more prominent Sufi scholar in Aceh, al-Singkili (d.1693), who established a school of mysticism contributing to the spread of the Shattariyya order in Indonesia, even though the order did not survive in the Arabian Peninsula.[167] Shattariya is primarily identified with the Malay people, so it could be considered somewhat nationalist,[168] but there is also unmistakable Hindu influence in the Shattariya of Indonesia.[169] There are, then, four orders of Sufism most influential in the development of Islam in Indonesia—the Shattariyya, Qadiriyya, Wujudiyya, and Naqshbandiyya. As a side note, over time, elite Jawi mysticism shifted from regally sponsored Shattariyya to reformist Naqshbandiyya and, ultimately, to rationalist Cairene Salafiyya.[170]

"The influence of Islam was not unidirectional from the Middle East to Southeast Asia, because there are fourteenth century Arabic sources that present prominent Arab figures as disciples of Muslim scholars hailing from, or associated with, the Indonesian archipelago."[171] There was a community of Malay in Mecca that ensured Indonesia was in touch with happenings in the Arab world. There have also been Malay communities at important spots on the popular trade routes that often integrated with the local societies.

"Well known in South India is the lineage of the seventeenth-century Sufi mystic sheikh Sadaqatullah of Kayalpattinam, whose tomb continues to attract devotees from Malaysia and Indonesia. Members of the Arab and Malay communities intermarried as with

---

[167] Ibid., 126.
[168] Laffan, *Islam*, 173.
[169] Ibid., 195.
[170] Ibid., 184.
[171] Ricci, 12, footnote 24.

the Maraikkayar, claiming descent from Arab seafarers, preferring intermarriage with the Muslims of the Archipelago over marriage with the lower strata of Tamil Muslim society."[172]

Even with the strong tradition of Sufism in the early years of Islam in Indonesia, this was not to last. As with the process of Islamization in India, this slow process of accretion of Sufi teachings and Popular Sufism were soon met with the "correction" of reform.

---

[172] Ibid., 9.

VIII

REFORMISM AND TRADITIONALISM

The reform movement was prominent in the 18th and 19th centuries in Southeast Asia and has continued unto the present day, with its greatest influence during the past 50 years. The lack of Sufi exegetical material on the Quran in the 15th to 17th century is surprising since the previous centuries were dominated by it. This may be because the Sufi-leaning narrative commentaries were for the masses, and as the educated religious elite became more established, the narratives declined. Also, significant amounts of monistic Sufi exegetical material was destroyed by al-Raniri and his followers. Even so, the pluralistic nature of Islam and the vast influence of Sufism continue to ensure that there is not just one version of Islam.

The reformist movements originated and gained ground in Arabia, and the effects were felt throughout the Muslim world. As transportation to Mecca improved, more and more Muslims in Southeast Asia were affected by the teachings of Arab Muslims through the increased presence of Hadrami Arabs in South and Southeast Asia, and through increased opportunity for travel to Arabia on the *hajj*.[173] As Indonesian Muslims were

---

[173] Tagliacozzo, Eric. *The Longest Journey: Southeast Asians and the Pilgrimage to Mecca*. (New York: Oxford University Press, 2013). Kindle Electronic Edition.

exposed more to the Middle East, many were increasingly convinced of the need for reform. "Muslims in Southeast Asia participated in networks of sheikhs, Sufi gurus, theologians, reformers, and disciples from across the Muslim world who converged on Mecca for the hajj pilgrimage and often for longer periods of residence and study. Well known is the fact that the neighborhood of Southeast Asians in the sacred city, known as Kampong Jawah (in today's Malaysia), contained the largest of any visiting groups in the mid nineteenth century, and no language besides Arabic was as widely understood at the time as Malay."[174]

Most of the Arabs in South and Southeast Asia adhere to the Shafi'i school of Islam and Sufi-inspired practices. Shafi'i was closely tied to the Islamic semi-rationalist approach to theology (*kalam*) associated with Ashari, and has become one of the four major schools in Islam today, with most adherents found in East Africa and Indonesia because of Sufi Shafi'i seagoing scholars from the Hadhramaut.[175] There were several migrations of Hadramis, first because of drought and tribal wars at home, but also for trading opportunities. In the early centuries of migration the most common traveler was a man who was both a trader and a religious missionary, most often from the Sada group (or *sayyid*, meaning "a descendent of Muhammad"). There were also poor Hadramis, from non-Sada groups, who traveled to fill the various labor needs within the global economy of the nineteenth century.[176] Over time they became more integrated into Malay communities, often through intermarriage, and so turned out to be essentially Malay.[177]

It is important to keep in mind the small-group and decentralized nature of Sufism to help better understand why its

---

[174] Ricci, 17-18.

[175] Anne K. Bang, *Sufis and Scholars of the Sea: Family Networks in East Africa, 1860-1925* (London: RoutledgeCurzon, 2003), 114.

[176] Leif Manger, *The Hadrami Diaspora: Community-Building on the Indian Ocean Rim* (New York: Berghahn Books, 2010), 1.

[177] Ibid., 34-37.

practitioners have been so subject to persecution in the past and why Sufism does not usually generate a large political movement speaking with one voice. Sufis are also more concerned with spiritual things, and not the material world, and so they are not as outspoken and rigid as those espousing purely orthodox Islamic beliefs. Even so, Sufism has caused political concern, and Sufis even led uprisings against the Dutch colonial government, their insurrections facilitated by the large followings associated with some *tarekat* (Sufi brotherhoods).[178] In colonial Indonesia, the *tarekat* were seen as a possible threat, and in some cases purely orthodox Islam was preferred. Many modernists in Indonesia even supported the ascent in Arabia of the Saudi dynasty because of their shared distaste for the alleged excesses of the Sufi *shaykh*.[179]

The general perception of the "goodness" or "badness" of Sufi gurus (teachers) and orders usually depended on the individual *shaykh*. The Dutch Islamist Snouck Hurgronje observed that if a guru:

> "is stupid and bad, then he teaches the superstitious villager not so much to be a good and religious person as to do his every bidding; indeed there are even some who teach thieves the arts of invisibility or invulnerability for missions that they have planned against others. If he is ignorant without malicious intentions, then he teaches false magical arts, or such things that his students will not understand, and about which he himself has little idea. A clever and good *tarekat* teacher, meanwhile, directs the people, to the best of his knowledge, on the path of religion, such that they will have a greater influence upon the hearts [of the people] than the [normal] kitab (holy book) teacher…The population treats the instructions of

---

[178] Pringle, 33.
[179] Michael Laffan, "National Crisis and the Representation of traditional Sufism in Indonesia: The Periodicals *Salafy* and *Sufi*" in *Sufism and the 'Modern' in Islam* edited by Martin van Bruinessen and Julia Day Howell (New York: I.B. Tauris & Co Ltd, 2007), 149.

clever teachers almost as if they were divine."[180]

In a letter written in 1904, Snouck Hurgronje also identified certain mystic teachers and their writings as "absolutely safe, viewed from the political standpoint; this mysticism even accords a greater place to humanitarian and tolerant concepts than orthodox Islam does." This first Western scholar of Islam who undertook a profound study of Islamic Law also showed himself to be an outspoken defender of Islamic mysticism.[181]

Many thought that Sufism would not last until the modern era, but this has not been the case, as Sufism has been very capable of adapting. Sufi communities are seen throughout the world, and they often feature singing as a part of their worship, an activity usually identified as "extreme" within Islam. And then there are the efforts to enter a trance-like state through rituals or other means, a practice referred to as *dhikr*, or remembrance.[182] The best known of these observances are associated with the whirling dervishes of Turkey.

The traditional organization of Sufi orders, or *tariqa* (Indonesian *tarekat*), was a major factor leading to the judgment that Sufism was not suitable for modernity, but this social expression of the faith has been remarkably flexible and continues to be a means for informal leaders to exercise moral authority among their disciples in countries like Egypt[183] and Indonesia.[184] Before the eighteenth century most orders were not self-supporting social organizations, but rather allied themselves with other groups. In the countryside they became embedded in

[180] Laffan, *Islam*, 156.
[181] Karel Steenbrink, "Opposition to Islamic Mysticism in Nineteenth-Century Indonesia" in *Islamic Mysticism Contested: Thirteen Centuries of Controversies and Polemics* edited by Frederick de Jong and Bernd Radtke (Leiden: Brill, 1999), 703-704.
[182] Riddell, *Islam*, 76-77.
[183] Rachida Chih, "What is a Sufi Order? Revisiting the Concept through a Case Study of the Khalwatiyya in Contemporary Egypt" in *Sufism and the 'Modern' in Islam* edited by Martin van Bruinessen and Julia Day Howell (New York: I.B. Tauris & Co Ltd, 2007), 21-38.
[184] Laffan, "National," 162-171.

families and clans and also regional units, which a *shaykh* was able to manipulate through their charismatic power. In urban societies the orders were linked to the trade guilds, and in the Ottoman Empire, Sufis allied themselves with military units.[185] Since *tariqa* (Sufi brotherhoods) were important in the various structures of popular Islam, their place in society has changed as popular culture itself has changed. Different types of *tariqa* have found ways to become effective organizations in contemporary societies. Building on established traditions and existing associational networks, *tariqa* have often emerged as more effective "modern associations" than organizations structured in a more explicitly modern manner. An important case study of this is in the modern state of Turkey, where *tariqa* (brotherhoods) were banned, but continue to survive in the context of legal secularism.[186]

While the Sufi orders are adapting to the modern world, the practices of Popular Sufism often remain the same. These non-standard varieties of Islam throughout Indonesia may have some elements in common. In Java, Indonesia, these approaches are referred to, collectively, as *abangan* Islam, and are fairly representative of local varieties found throughout the nation's islands. They are not merely counted as "inobservant Islam," but as traditions of religious knowledge with their own rituals, cosmology, and customs. As Robert Hefner explains,

> "It is also not sufficient to say that they are Hindu or Buddhist at the core, because there are powerful influences of popular varieties of Sufism and pantheistic mysticism. Even so, the practitioners see themselves as Muslims, conceding that it was an Islam of an ethnicized variety. As a result, there are several points of intellectual

---

[185] Levtzion, 149.

[186] John O. Voll, "Contemporary Sufism and Current Social Theory" in *Sufism and the 'Modern' in Islam* edited by Martin van Bruinessen and Julia Day Howell (New York: I.B. Tauris & Co Ltd, 2007), 286-289.

and practical linkage between the Sunni standard and the *abangan* variety. This is usually seen in that the prayers of rituals make reference to Allah and the Prophet Muhammad, but then go on to invoke the presence of spirits of a less Islamic nature."[187]

Hefner continues,

"These spirits could usually be categorized as ancestral or guardian in nature, and through prayer, offerings, and incense could be drawn for blessed effect (*barakah*; Ind., *berkat*) into this world. There was also usually a space in communities that served as a point of passage from the village to a supernatural world seen as, not distant and otherworldly, but accessible from the world of the living. These spaces were often centered on the graves of saint-like ancestors, who were often the village's human founders, usually represented as a male and a female. These sites could then be assimilated to the status of a Sufi *kramat*, which is a burial place for venerating the soul of a deceased Muslim saint. Rituals usually include the presentation of food offerings at the site, as well as a village elder reciting a short Arabic prayer and a prayer in the local language. After the invoked spirits consumed the invisible essence (*sari*) of the food offerings, the physical residue of which, blessed by the spirits' presence, is then taken home to be shared among members of the family."[188]

But there are limits to these improvisations:

"On the other hand, there were some ritual events, such as funerary rites, which were considered a straightforward

---

[187] Hefner, "*abangan*," 74.
[188] Ibid., 75-76.

Islamic affair, and the path was described in exclusively Islamic terms. Even this local religious knowledge was referred to as *ilmu* or 'esoteric knowledge' (Ar. *'ilm*), the same term as used for the Islamic sciences studied at Islamic religious schools. This *abangan ilmu* was unfinished, open, and additive, rather than fixed, exclusive, and scripturalist."[189]

These non-standard forms of Islam currently face a common struggle in that they are "swimming against a fierce normative tide" to conform throughout Indonesia.[190] In Java, the local practices of Popular Sufism or *abangan* Islam are in serious decline, but in some of the more remote areas of Indonesia they are still strong.

The Sufi nature of the Islam that took root in Indonesia points to why the people would have been drawn to it spiritually, and how they saw it as beneficial in bringing more organization and solidarity to their often-disjointed kingdoms. The flexible and mystical nature of Sufism was not only appealing to the masses,[191] but initially took root within the elite and was used by kings and sultans to affirm their status of being above the law and knowing more than the common people. Popular Sufism allowed Islam to adapt to the pre-Islamic practices of Indonesia, while the Sufi brotherhoods allowed key individuals to hold special rank and influence within the context of the world religion of Islam. As Islam gained prominence through the prosperity of Arab and Indian traders and through its ability to unite the people of Indonesia against colonial powers, the fact that it could also be mystical in nature allowed it to find wide acceptance. Out of the many factors that led to Islamization in Indonesia, the fact that Islam had mystical Sufi traditions, along with a written core to

---

[189] Ibid., 77-78.
[190] Ibid., 74.
[191] Sherman A. Jackson, *Sufism for Non-Sufis: Ibn Ata Allah al-Sakandari's Taj al-Arus* (Oxford: Oxford University Press, 2012), 4.

facilitate unity with a global community, probably enabled it to become the majority religion of the archipelago. Some Indian Sufi scholars were concerned with orthodoxy, and wrote treatises such as the *Tuhfa*. These scholars were crucial in the development of Sufi thought in Indonesia and the wide acceptance of concepts such as the seven grades of being (*martabat tujuh*).[192] The path of the Sufis engulfed the world faster than the political spread of Islam.[193] These traditions that began so long ago still show their appeal and vitality today in the beliefs and practices of Muslims throughout Indonesia and the world.

---

[192] A.H. Johns, *The Gift Addressed to the Spirit of the Prophet (al-Tuhfa al-mursala ila ruh al-nabi)* (Canberra: The Australian National University, 1965), 8.

[193] Neeru Misra, "Sufism: The Social Bond in Medieval India" in Misra, 10.

IX

MYSTICISM ON BUTON

The former kingdom (and eventually sultanate) of Buton has a long tradition of mysticism and Sufism among its people and its rulers reaching back to the 16th century. A look at Sufism on this island provides a good case study to see how a variety of teachings of Sufi orders in the past, as well as elements of Popular Sufism, have found their way to remote areas and in many ways still persist today. As the scholar Nicholson noted, "Mysticism is such a vital element in Islam that without some understanding of its ideas and of the forms which they assume we should seek in vain to penetrate below the surface of Muslim religious life."[194]

The sixth ruler of Buton, Murhum, was the first ruler of the kingdom to accept Islam. (He was given the title of "sultan" by Sheik Abd al-Wahid). As recounted earlier in the book, according to the traditions of Buton, Islam was brought to Buton by an Arab from Gujarat named Abdul Wahid, who represented Sufi teachings that came out of Johor, Malaysia. He landed in Burangasi around the year 1527 after earlier stopping in Johor. His second visit was reportedly in 1542 according to the Butonese historian Zahari, but Pim Schoorl believes it was

---

[194] Nicholson, vi.

1540.[195] This second visit was when Buton officially accepted Islam and became a sultanate, though there are several versions of this story.

Early in the process of the acceptance of Islam among these islands, mysticism or Sufism (also called *tasawuf*), played a very large role in the laws and practices of the faith in Buton. Even until the end of the 17th century, *tasawuf* was pre-eminent when compared with Islam *fikih* (Muslim canonical jurisprudence). The manuscripts that remain of the sultanate of Buton are dominated by *tasawuf* teachings,[196] with Sultan Muhammad Aydarus (r. 1824-1851) authoring many works on Sufism.[197] Specific Sufi orders that various sultans adhered to from the seventeenth to the nineteenth century include Qadiriyya, Shattariya, Sammaniyya, and Naqshbandiyya.[198] There are several examples of syncretism between the Hindu-Buddhist culture of pre-Islamic Buton and the teachings of Islam because of the philosophy of *pata palena*, that "life is in the realm of ideas (thoughts)". This focus on things that cannot be seen and things spiritual has been a major influence on the beliefs of the Butonese. One of the most notable is that of the *rohi polimba*, or "moving spirit," which can be described as reincarnation, but with a mystical Islamic twist. In Komberi, East Buton, there are wooden graveside poles (*mayasa*) that seem to illustrate a human spirit's movement after death in the fourth realm of *arwah*. According to some people on Buton, certain individuals have the ability to send their spirits after death

---

[195] Tawalinuddin Haris, "Benteng Keraton Buton," in *Monumen: karya persembahan untuk Prof. Dr. R. Soekmono*, eds. Edi Sedyawati and Ingrid H.E. Pojoh (Depok: Fakultas Sastra, Universitas Indonesia, 1990), 325-328.

[196] Abd. Rahim Yunus, *Ajaran Islam Yang Dominan Dalam Naskah Peninggalan Kesultanan Buton* (Ujungpandang: Pusat Penelitian Iain Alauddin, 1996/1997), 1-4.

[197] A.C.S. Peacock, "Arabic Manuscripts from Buton, Southeast Sulawesi, and the Literary Activities of Sultan Muhammad Aydarus (1824-1851)" *Journal of Islamic Manuscripts* 10 (2019): 52-53; Hasaruddin & Andi Tenri Machmud, "Peranan Sultan dalam Pengembangan Tradisi Tulis di Kesultanan Buton" *Jumantara* 3, no. 2 (2012): 91.

[198] Yunus, *Tasawuf*, 51-66, 72-74.

into the womb of a woman to be born again as another child.[199] In this vein, elements of Butonese cultural beliefs and symbols are present in most all rituals and events on the island, even if these are Islamic in nature.[200]

During the mid-sixteenth century, Sufi teachings that put great importance on the need for harmony and unity in the universe were developing. It called for meditation on the relationship between mankind and God, appealing to the five grades of being first developed by Ibn al-Arabi. Hamzah al-Fansuri played an important role in the dissemination of the grades of being in Indonesia, but Shams al-Din was instrumental in the doctrinal shift of al-Jili's five grades of being to the seven grades accepted by the Shattariya and Naqshbandiyya.[201] This teaching influenced the islands that now form Indonesia for hundreds of years, and even later in the 18th century, at least one Sumatran scholar urged that books about the seven grades be kept out of reach of unqualified people because of the "Malay" tendency to place themselves above the sharia.[202]

An example of Sufi literature making a lasting impact on the Sultanate of Buton is the Gujarati Muhammad ibn Fad-al-Burhanpuri's *The Gift Addressed to the Spirit of the Prophet*, which explains the seven grades of being, or *martabat tujuh*, which was written in 1590.[203] This concept played an important role in the organization of castes involved in the aristocracy of the Sultanate of Buton.[204] As part of the leadership of the Sultanate of Buton the *Sarana Wolio* was impacted by the Sufi Wujudiyya teachings

---

[199] J. W. (Pim) Schoorl, "Belief in reincarnation on Buton, S.E. Sulawesi, Indonesia." *Bijdragen tot de Taal-, Land- en Volkenkunde* 141 (1985): 103-134. [Indonesian translation published in *Masyarakat, Sejarah dan Budaya Buton*]; *Masyarakat, Sejarah, dan Budaya Buton* (Jakarta: Penerbit Djambatan bekerjasama dengan Perwakilan KITLV-Jakarta, 2003), 161-210.

[200] Haliadi, *Buton Islam dan Islam Buton: Islamisasi, Kolonialisme, dan Sinkretisme Agama* (Yogyakarta: Yayasan untuk Indonesia, 2000), 298-299.

[201] Laffan, *Islam*, 13.

[202] Ibid., 29.

[203] Johns.

[204] Yunus, *Tasawuf*, 67-68.

and the systematic cosmology of *martabat tujuh* became the constitution of the Sultanate of Buton.[205] The first version of this constitution was developed during the reign of the fourth sultan, La Elangi (1578-1615), also known as Dayanu Ikhsanuddin, with help from the Arabian religious expert Syarif Muhammed.[206] While there are mystical Sufi elements in this constitution, it deals primarily with practical matters pertaining to the government of the sultanate and also contains elements of more formal Islamic Law (*fiqh*) and Butonese culture.[207] This Sufi teaching of the seven grades of being (*martabat tujuh*) was used to legitimize the political system of the sultanate (see table below[208]). The four grades of being that did not deal directly with the unity of Allah were used to classify the four layers (or castes) of individuals in the kingdom: the king, the aristocracy, the common people, and the slaves—an extreme example of the indigenization of Sufi teachings in Indonesia.[209] Some of the teachings associated with these levels of being were believed to affect one's ability to control the weather and prevent natural disasters, the type of things that a Sultan of Buton was expected to manage. And drawing on Sufi insights and symbols the Sultan infused the design of his palace and fortress with deeper meaning.[210]

---

[205] Zahari 3-4.

[206] Schoorl, *Masyarakat*, 175.

[207] Muhammad Roy Purwanto, "Acculturation among Local Wisdom, Law and Sufism in Forming Martabat Tujuh Enactment of Buton Sultanate," *International Journal of Humanities and Management Sciences (IJHMS)* 4, no. 3 (2016): 289-290.

[208] Hans Bakker, "Consolidation of the Colonial State in the Sultanate of Buton: Historical Notes and Sociological Considerations" (Paper for the Conference on the Late Colonial State in Indonesia, NIAS, Wassenaar, 12-14 June 1989), 4.

[209] Martin van Bruinessen, *Kitab Kuning, Pesantren dan Tarekat* (Yogyakarta: Gading Publishing, 2012), 465-466.

[210] Mudjur Muif Ahmad Mudjriddin, *Mengungkap Tabir Sejarah Spiritual dan Metafisika, Theokrasi, serta Monarkhi Parlementer Kesulthanan Buton (Bidaaril Buthuunii)* (Bogor: Yayasan Jabbal Qubais, 2009); Mudjur Muif Ahmad Mudjriddin, *Benteng Keraton Kesultanan Buton: Monumen Sejarah Peradaban* (Bogor: Lembaga Pengkajian Budaya Buton, 2010).

Level	Societal Categories in Butonese Sultanate	Butonese Term (*Wolio*)
1.	Slaves	*batua*
2.	Commoners (Villagers)	*papara*
3.	Other Free Citizens	*maradika*
4.	Demoted Lower Nobility	*limbo*
5.	Lower Nobility	*walaka*
6.	Demoted Royalty, High Nobles	*analalaki*
7.	Royalty	*kaomu*

Today the deeper meanings of certain symbols and practices on Buton are considered secrets that only the older men in villages possess, and the younger generation is often hesitant to communicate them because of the risk of getting the story wrong and possibly incurring the wrath of certain mystical powers or a village elder. It can be difficult to differentiate which practices are pre-Islamic Butonese, and which originated from mystical Islam.[211] In general, rituals and beliefs related to fertility symbols found in rock formations (and boats) and the calling forth of ancestors are probably pre-Islamic, but even these are often combined with mystical Islamic concepts.[212] There is a growing amount of pressure for the leadership of villages throughout the island of Buton to conform to the will of modernist reformist Islam and erase some of the rituals that have been practiced for generations.[213] The result is often that the original meaning of these rituals is lost on the younger generation that takes part in the sanitized remnants. The older men and women in the villages are the guardians of this deeper meaning and will need to pass on these techniques and beliefs or they could eventually disappear.

---

[211] Tasrifin Tahara, *Melawan Stereotip: Etnografi, Reproduksi Identitas, dan Dinamika Masyarakat Katobengke Buton yang Terabaikan* (Jakarta: Kepustakaan Populer Gramedia, 2015), 150-153.
[212] Southon, 129, footnote 25.
[213] Palmer, 217-219.

Even with this declining influence, there are several elements of Sufism still seen in Buton today in the rituals the people conduct and the stories they tell. When conversations turn to the commonality of all humanity, regardless of national origin, the person of Adam arises as the father of all. In that connection, in Sufi teaching one of the grades of being is return to the state of Adam, which is also one of the goals of fasting during the month of Ramadan. Falling into trances and possession (*dhikr*) is not quite as prevalent today, but there is at least one annual ritual, practiced on Mt. Siontapina on Buton, where ancestors are believed to possess individuals, sometimes putting them in a trance-like state. These rituals are practiced close to the site of the grave of a powerful sultan in Buton's history, *Oputa Yi Koo*, and the ground surrounding the grave is seen as holy, or *keramat*.[214] Grave veneration of past saints is seen throughout Buton and Indonesia, where people go to pray for spiritual power and blessing. Among Muslims, Modernist and Salafi versions of Islam eschew this praying for power at gravesites, but it is very prevalent throughout the Muslim world and is often tied with Sufism.[215] Other means of obtaining power are through the drinking of written passages of the Quran that have been torn up and put in water, as well as through certain types of martial arts identified as Islamic.[216]

The advice and practices of medicine men, or *dukun*, often involve the creation and use of amulets, which used to be the realm of a *shaykh*. There are many stories of great men of the past (and canoes) who could close their eyes and travel great distances, as

---

[214] Caleb Coppenger, *The Mysteries of the Islands of Buton* (San Diego: Aventine Press, 2011).
[215] Palmer, 199, footnote 4; Martin Slama, "From Wali Songo to Wali Pitu: The Travelling of Islamic Saint Veneration to Bali," in *Between Harmony and Discrimination: Negotiating Religious Identities within Majority-Minority Relationships in Bali and Lombok* edited by Brigitta Hauser-Schaublin & David D. Harnish (Leiden: Brill, 2014), 114-117.
[216] Knysh, 53-57.

from Buton to Ternate or Mecca to conduct their daily prayers.[217] This resonates with the teachings on Muhammad and his night journey to Jerusalem. Also, the possibility of sinlessness in man is often attributed to past saints, a notion that probably found its origins in the teachings of the Perfect Man, which developed in Sufism around the person of Muhammad.[218]

Buton, as in other cultures around the world, have many who believe they live at the spot from which the world was created and that they are the guardians of the true Islamic teaching, which is often very mystical and secret, as in the Sufi orders of the past. Asia has many of its own that "reject the idea of the Middle East as the *de facto* "center" of Islam in the modern world."[219] The name Buton is said to come from the Arabic word *butuni*, which means stomach or womb, referring to the place where the core teachings are held. This symbolism, using the human body with the stomach as its core, is also connected to the shape of the island, as well as to the shape of some Arabic letters.[220] These are just a few of the ways that Sufi teachings and tendencies have survived today, even though they have not been closely guarded and passed down through Sufi orders as in the past. There are still individuals who hold *shaykh*-like status today, though they are usually referred to as *dukun* or those with powerful *ilmu* (esoteric knowledge).

Most of these deeper, secret, and mystical teachings that are found throughout the Muslim world cannot all be written down in a cohesive and comprehensive way because of their varied nature depending on where they are found and the individual that is communicating them. This book attempted to provide

---

[217] Southon, 17.
[218] Carool Kersten, *History of Islam in Indonesia: Unity in Diversity* (Edinburgh: Edinburgh University Press, 2017), location 733.
[219] Terenjit Sevea, "Making Medinas in the East: Islamist Connections and Progressive Islam," in *Islamic Connections: Muslim Societies in South and Southeast Asia* edited by R. Michael Feener and Terenjit Sevea (Singapore: Institute of Southeast Asian Studies (ISEAS), 2009), 150.
[220] Knysh, 53-57.

some clues to the origin of the mystical Islamic teachings on Buton as well as argue that they cannot be dismissed as local "folk Islam." Mysticism and traditionalism within Islam is still the way of life for a large part of the Muslim world and cannot be dismissed as outdated and backwards. It is a vibrant part of Islam today and has kept the peace in many parts of the world where more modern forms of Islam have caused strife. Even though it may be hard to communicate all the teachings of mysticism in Islam, many aspects of this ancient faith have been preserved in the "womb" of Buton. Visits to the Regencies of South Buton, Buton, and the city of Baubau today can provide clues to the ways that Muslims still live and communicate in a much more hospitable and warm way than is usually portrayed in news reports in the United States and other countries of the West. Visit South Buton today to see for yourself! The people will be happy to receive you and discuss the deeper truths of what it means to be human and the variety of ways that people of different cultures in the world try and connect with their Creator.

BIBLIOGRAPHY

Ahmed, Shahab. *What is Islam? The Importance of Being Islamic*. Princeton: Princeton University Press, 2016. Kindle Electronic Edition.

Andaya, Leonard. *The World of Maluku: Eastern Indonesia in the Early Modern Period*. Honolulu: University of Hawai'i Press, 1993.

al-Arabi. *The Ringstones of Wisdom (Fusus al-hikam)*, translated by Caner K. Dagli. Chicago: Great Books of the Islamic World, 2004.

Azra, Azyumardi. *.Islam in the Indonesian World: An Account of Institutional Formation*. Bandung: Mizan Pustaka, 2006.

_____. "Opposition to Sufism in the East Indies in the Seventeenth and Eighteenth Centuries." In Jong, 665-686.

_____.*The Origins of Islamic Reformism in Southeast Asia: Networks of Malay-Indonesian and Middle Eastern 'Ulama' in the Seventeenth and Eighteenth Centuries*. Honolulu: University of Hawai'i Press, 2004.

Bakker, Hans. "Consolidation of the Colonial State in the Sultanate of Buton: Historical Notes and Sociological Considerations." Paper for the Conference on the Late

Colonial State in Indonesia, NIAS, Wassenaar, 12-14 June 1989.

Baldick, Julian. *Mystical Islam: An Introduction to Sufism.* London: I.B. Tauris and Co. Ltd., 1989.

Bang, Anne K. *Sufis and Scholars of the Sea: Family Networks in East Africa, 1860-1925.* London: RoutledgeCurzon, 2003.

Barfield, Thomas J. "Turk, Persian, and Arab: Changing Relationships between Tribes and State in Iran and along Its Frontiers." In Keddie, 61-88.

Barton, Greg. "Islam and Democratic Transition in Indonesia." In Cheng, 221-241.

Boland, J. *The Struggle of Islam in Modern Indonesia.* The Hague: Martinus Nijhoff, 1971.

Bowen, John R. *Islam, Law and Equality in Indonesia: An Anthropology of Public Reasoning.* Cambridge: Cambridge University Press, 2003.

Bruinessen, Martin van, ed. *Contemporary Developments in Indonesian Islam: Explaining the "Conservative Turn."* Singapore: Institute of Southeast Asian Studies (ISEAS), 2013.

_____. *Kitab Kuning, Pesantren dan Tarekat.* Yogyakarta: Gading Publishing, 2012.

_____. "Sufism, 'Popular' Islam and the Encounter with Modernity," in Masud, 125-157.

_____ and Julia Day Howell. *Sufism and the 'Modern' in Islam.* New York: I.B. Tauris &Co Ltd, 2007. Cahill, Thomas. *Heretics and Heroes: How Renaissance Artists and Reformation Priests Created Our World.* New York: Random House/Anchor, 2013.

Cederroth, Sven. "Indonesia and Malaysia." In Westerlund, 253-277.

Cheng, Tun-Jen and Deborah A. Brown, eds. *Religious Organizations and Democratization: Case Studies from Contemporary Asia.* Armonk: M.E. Sharpe, Inc., 2006.

Chih, Rachida. "What is a Sufi Order? Revisiting the Concept through a Case Study of the Khalwatiyya in Contemporary Egypt." In Bruinessen, 21-38.

Chittick, William C. *Imaginal Worlds: Ibn al-'Arabi and the Problem of Religious Diversity.* New York: State University of New York Press, 1994.

Coppenger, Caleb. *The Mysteries of the Islands of Buton.* San Diego: Aventine Press, 2011.

Dale, Stephen F. *The Muslim Empires of the Ottomans, Safavids, and Mughals.* New York: Cambridge University Press, 2010.

Doorn-Harder, Pieternella van. *Women Shaping Islam: Indonesian Women Reading the Quran.* Urbana: University of Illinois Press, 2006.

Durie, Mark. *The Third Choice: Islam, Dhimmitude, and Freedom.* Deror Books, 2010.

Eaton, Richard M. "Approaches to the Study of Conversion to Islam in India." In Lorenzen, 105-127.

Feener, R. Michael and Terenjit Sevea, eds. *Islamic Connections: Muslim Societies in South and Southeast Asia.* Singapore: Institute of Southeast Asian Studies (ISEAS), 2009.

_____. "Issues and Ideologies in the Study of Regional Muslim Cultures." In Feener, *Connections*, xiii-xxiii.

Feillard, Andree and Remy Madinier. *The End of Innocence? Indonesian Islam and the Temptations of Radicalism.* Singapore: National University of Singapore Press in association with IRASEC (a French Research Institute on Contemporary Southeast Asia), 2011.

_____. "Traditionalist Islam and the State in Indonesia: The Road to Legitimacy and Renewal" in Hefner, *Nation-States*, 149-150.

Filiu, Jean-Pierre, *Apocalypse in Islam*. Berkeley: University of California Press, 2011.

Flecker, Michael. "A Ninth-Century AD Arab or Indian Shipwreck in Indonesia: First Evidence for Direct Trade with China." *World Archaeology* 32, no.3 (February 2001): 335-354.

Geertz, Clifford. *Islam Observed: Religious Development in Morocco and Indonesia*. New Haven: Yale University Press, 1968.

Geoffroy, Eric. *Introduction to Sufism: The Inner Path of Islam*. Bloomington: World Wisdom, 2010.

al-Ghazali. *Inner Dimensions of Islamic Worship*. Translated from the *Ihya' 'Ulum al-Din* by Muhtar Holland. Leicestershire: The Islamic Foundation, 1983.

Glick, Thomas F. *Islamic and Christian Spain in the Early Middle Ages*. Princeton University Press, 1979.

Haliadi. *Buton Islam dan Islam Buton: Islamisasi, Kolonialisme, dan Sinkretisme Agama*. Yogyakarta: Yayasan untuk Indonesia, 2000.

Halm, Heinz. *Shi'ism* .Second Edition. New York: Columbia University Press, 2004.

Haris, Tawalinuddin. "Benteng Keraton Buton." In Sedyawati, 319-328.

Hasaruddin and Andi Tenri Machmud, "Peranan Sultan dalam Pengembangan Tradisi Tulis di Kesultanan Buton." *Jumantara* 3, no. 2 (2012): 89-104.

Hauser-Schaublin, Brigitta and David D. Harnish, eds. *Between Harmony and Discrimination: Negotiating Religious*

Identities within Majority-Minority Relationships in Bali and Lombok. Leiden: Brill, 2014.

Haykel, Bernard. "On the Nature of Salafi Thought and Action." In Meijer, 33-51.

Hefner, Robert W. and Patricia Horvatich, eds. *Islam in an Era of Nation-States: Politics and Religious Renewal in Muslim Southeast Asia*. Honolulu: University of Hawai'i Press, 1997.

──────. "Where have all the *abangan* gone?" In Picard, 71-91.

Jackson, Sherman A. *Sufism for Non-Sufis: Ibn Ata Allah al-Sakandari's Taj al-Arus*. Oxford: Oxford University Press, 2012.

Johns, A.H. *The Gift Addressed to the Spirit of the Prophet (al-Tuhfa al-mursala ila ruh al-nabi)*. Canberra: The Australian National University, 1965.

Jong, Frederick de and Bernd Radtke. *Islamic Mysticism Contested: Thirteen Centuries of Controversies and Polemics*. Leiden: Brill, 1999.

Karamustafa, Ahmet T. *Sufism: The Formative Period*. Edinburgh: Edinburgh University Press, 2007.

Karsh, Efraim. *Islamic Imperialism: A History*. New Haven: Yale University Press, 2006.

Keddie, Nikki R. and Rudi Matthee, eds. *Iran and the Surrounding World: Interactions in Culture and Cultural Politics*. Seattle: University of Washington Press, 2002.

Kennedy, Hugh. *The Court of the Caliphs: The Rise and Fall of Islam's Greatest Dynasty*. London: Weidenfeld & Nicolson, 2004.

Kersten, Carool. *History of Islam in Indonesia: Unity in Diversity* (The New Edinburgh Islamic Surveys). Edinburgh:

Edinburgh University Press, 2017. Kindle Electronic Edition.

Kiem, Christian. "Re-Islamization among Muslim Youth in Ternate Town." *Sojourn: Journal of Social Issues in Southeast Asia* 8, no. 1 (February 1993): 92-127.

Knysh, Alexander. *Sufism: A New History of Islamic Mysticism*. Princeton: Princeton University Press, 2017.

Laffan, Michael. "National Crisis and the Representation of traditional Sufism in Indonesia: The Periodicals *Salafy* and *Sufi*." In Bruinessen, 149-171.

_____. *The Makings of Indonesian Islam: Orientalism and the Narration of a Sufi Past*. Princeton: Princeton University Press, 2011.

Lav, Daniel. *Radical Islam and the Revival of Medieval Theology*. Cambridge: Cambridge University Press, 2012.

Levtzion, Nehemia. "Eighteenth Century Sufi Brotherhoods: Structural, Organizational and Ritual Changes." In Riddell, *Festschrift*, 147-160.

Lewisohn, Leonard, ed. *Heritage of Sufism: Classical Persian Sufism from its Origins to Rumi (700-1300)*, Vol. 1. Oxford: Oneworld Publications, 1999.

Lockard, Craig A. "The Sea Common to All: Maritime Frontiers, Port Cities, and Chinese Traders in the Southeast Asian Age of Commerce, ca. 1400-1750." *Journal of World History* 21, no. 2 (2010): 219-247.

Lorenzen, David N. *Religious Movements in South Asia 600-1800*. Delhi: Oxford University Press, 2004.

Manger, Leif. *The Hadrami Diaspora: Community-Building on the Indian Ocean Rim*. New York: Berghahn Books, 2010.

Marashi, Afshin. "The Nation's Poet: Ferdowsi and the Iranian National Imagination." In Atabaki, 93-111.

Masud, Muhammad Khalid, Armando Salvatore, and Martin van Bruinessen, eds. *Islam and Modernity: Key Issues and Debates*. Edinburgh: Edinburgh University Press, 2009.

Meijer, Roel, ed. *Global Salafism: Islam's New Religious Movement*. New York: Columbia University Press, 2009.

Misra, Neeru, ed. *Sufis and Sufism: Some Reflections*. New Delhi: Manohar Publishers, 2004.

_____. "Sufism: The Social Bond in Medieval India" in Misra, *Sufis*, 7-36.

Mudjriddin, Mudjur Muif Ahmad. *Mengungkap Tabir Sejarah Spiritual dan Metafisika, Theokrasi, serta Monarkhi Parlementer Kesulthanan Buton (Bidaaril Buthuunii)*. Bogor: Yayasan Jabbal Qubais, 2009.

_____.*Benteng Keraton Kesultanan Buton: Monumen Sejarah Peradaban* (Bogor: Lembaga Pengkajian Budaya Buton, 2010.

Murad, Khurram. "Foreword," in Al-Ghazali, 7-17.

Nasr, Seyyed Hossein. "The Rise and Development of Persian Sufism," in Lewisohn, 1-18.

Nicholson, Reynold A. *Studies in Islamic Mysticism*. Cambridge: Cambridge University Press, 1921.

Nourse, Jennifer W. "The meaning of *dukun* and allure of Sufi healers: How Persian cosmopolitans transformed Malay-Indonesian history." *Journal of Southeast Asian Studies* 44, no.3 (October 2013): 400-422.

Ohlander, Erik S. *Sufism in an Age of Transition: Umar al-Suhrawardi and the Rise of the Islamic Mystical Brotherhoods*. Leiden: Brill, 2008.

Palmer, Blair D. "Trading Traditions: Modernist Islam and Agricultural Rituals in Buton, Indonesia," in Reuter, 197-221 (Chapter 10).

Peacock, A.C.S. "Arabic Manuscripts from Buton, Southeast Sulawesi, and the Literary Activities of Sultan Muhammad Aydarus (1824-1851)." *Journal of Islamic Manuscripts* 10 (2019): 44-83.

Picard, Michel and Remy Madinier, eds. *The Politics of Religion in Indonesia*. London: Routledge, 2011.

Prange, Sebastian R. "Like Banners on the Sea: Muslim Trade Networks and Islamization in Malabar and Maritime Southeast Asia." In Feener, 25-47.

Pringle, Robert. *Understanding Islam in Indonesia: Politics and Diversity*. Honolulu: University of Hawai'i Press, 2010.

Purwanto, Muhammad Roy. "Acculturation among Local Wisdom, Law and Sufism in Forming Martabat Tujuh Enactment of Buton Sultanate." *International Journal of Humanities and Management Sciences (IJHMS)* 4, no. 3 (2016): 288-292.

Radtke, Bernd and John O'Kane. *The Concept of Sainthood in Early Islamic Mysticism: Two Works by Al-Hakim Al-Tirmidhi*. Surrey: Curzon Press, 1996.

Reid, Anthony. "Early Southeast Asian Categorizations of Europeans." In Schwartz, 268-294.

_____. "Islamization and Christianization in Southeast Asia: The Critical Phase, 1550-1650." In Reid, 151-179.

_____, ed. *Southeast Asia in the Early Modern Era: Trade, Power, and Belief*. Ithaca: Cornell University Press, 1993.

Renard, John. *Friends of God: Islamic Images of Piety, Commitment, and Servanthood*. Berkeley: University of California Press, 2008.

_____. *Historical Dictionary of Sufism*. Lanham, Maryland: The Scarecrow Press, Inc., 2005.

Reuter, Thomas & Alexander Horstmann, eds. *Faith in the future: understanding the revitalization of religions and cultural traditions in Asia*. Leiden: Brill, 2013.

Ricci, Ronit. *Islam Translated: Literature, Conversion, and the Arabic Cosmopolis of South and Southeast Asia*. Chicago: The University of Chicago Press, 2011.

Ricklefs, M.C. *A History of Modern Indonesia since c. 1200*, Fourth Edition. New York: Palgrave Macmillan, 2008. Kindle Electronic Edition.

Riddell, Peter G. "Arab Migrants and Islamization in the Malay World during the Colonial Period," in *Indonesia and the Malay World* 29, no. 84 (2001): 113-125.

_____. *Islam and the Malay-Indonesian World: Transmission and Responses*. Honolulu: University of Hawai'i Press, 2001.

_____ and Tony Street, eds. *Islam: Essays on Scripture, Thought and Society: A Festschrift in Honour of Anthony H. Johns*. Leiden: Brill, 1997.

Riyadi, Abdul Kadir. *Arkeologi Tasawuf: Melacak Jejak Pemikiran Tasawuf dari Al-Muhasibi hingga Tasawuf Nusantara*. Bandung: Mizan, 2016.

Saleh, Fauzan. *Modern Trends in Islamic Theological Discourse in 20th Century Indonesia: A Critical Survey*. Leiden: Brill, 2001.

Schoorl, J. W. (Pim). "Belief in reincarnation on Buton, S.E. Sulawesi, Indonesia." *Bijdragen tot de Taal-, Land- en Volkenkunde* 141 (1985): 103-134. [Indonesian translation published in *Masyarakat, Sejarah dan Budaya Buton*]

_____. *Masyarakat, Sejarah, dan Budaya Buton*. Jakarta: Penerbit Djambatan bekerjasama dengan Perwakilan KITLV-Jakarta, 2003.

Sedyawati, Edi and Ingrid H.E. Pojoh, eds. *Monumen: karya persembahan untuk Prof. Dr. R. Soekmono.* Depok: Fakultas Sastra, Universitas Indonesia, 1990.

Sevea, Terenjit. "Making Medinas in the East: Islamist Connections and Progressive Islam." In Feener, *Connections*, 149-174.

Slama, Martin. "From Wali Songo to Wali Pitu: The Travelling of Islamic Saint Veneration to Bali." In Hauser-Schaublin, 112-143 (Chapter 4).

Southon, Michael. "The navel of the perahu: meaning and values in the maritime trading economy of a Butonese village." Master's Thesis, Australian National University, 1994.

Steenbrink, Karel. "Opposition to Islamic Mysticism in Nineteenth-Century Indonesia." In Jong, 687-704.

Tagliacozzo, Eric. *The Longest Journey: Southeast Asians and the Pilgrimage to Mecca.* New York: Oxford University Press, 2013. Kindle Electronic Edition.

Tahara, Tasrifin. *Melawan Stereotip: Etnografi, Reproduksi Identitas, dan Dinamika Masyarakat Katobengke Buton yang Terabaikan.* Jakarta: Kepustakaan Populer Gramedia, 2015.

Thohari, Hajriyanto Y., Fuad Fanani Ahmad, Andar Nubowo, and Muhd. Abdullah Darraz. *Becoming Muhammadiyah: Autobiografi Gerakan Kaum Islam Berkemajuan.* Bandung: Mizan, 2016.

Trimingham, J. Spencer. *The Sufi Orders in Islam.* London: Oxford University Press, 1971.

Unknown, "Iranian Contributions to Islamic Culture," 150-174.

Voll, John O. "Contemporary Sufism and Current Social Theory." In Bruinessen, 281-298.

Yunus, Abd. Rahim. *Ajaran Islam Yang Dominan Dalam Naskah Peninggalan Kesultanan Buton*. Ujungpandang: Pusat Penelitian Iain Alauddin, 1996/1997.

_____. *Posisi Tasawuf Dalam Sistem Kekuasaan di Kesultanan Buton Pada Abad Ke-19*. Jakarta: Indonesian-Netherlands Cooperation in Islamic Studies (INIS), 1995.

Zahari, Abdul Mulku. *Katalog naskah Buton koleksi Abdul Mulku Zahari*. Compiled by Achadiati Ikram. Yayasan Obor Indonesia, 2002.

Significant Empires and Sultanates

- Persian Empire (Iran), 550 BC – 651 AD
- Byzantine Empire (Turkey), 395 – 641 AD
- "Rightly Guided" Caliphs (Arabia), 632-661
- Umayyad Caliphate (Damascus, Syria), 661-750
  - Al-Andalus (Spain), 756-929
- Abbasid Caliphate (Baghdad, Iraq), 750-1258
- Mongol Empire (from Mongolia), 1206-1368
- Ternate Sultanate (Maluku, Indonesia), 1257-1914
- Malacca Sultanate (Malaysia), 1400-1511
- Ottoman Empire (Turkey), 1453-1922
  - Mamluk Sultanate (North Africa), 1250-1517
  - Aceh Sultanate (Sumatra, Indonesia), 1496-1903
  - Mughal Empire (India), 1526-1857
- Demak Sultanate (Java, Indonesia), 1475-1554
- Safavid Dynasty (Iran, Shi'a), 1501-1736
- Buton Sultanate (Baubau, Indonesia), 1540-1961

Types of Islamic Law (Fiqh)

Sunni Jurisprudence (*Madhhab*)
- North, Central, and West Africa (*Maliki*)
- Turkey, Central Asia, Afghanistan, and Pakistan (*Hanafi*)
- Saudi Arabia, Kuwait, and Qatar (*Hanbali*)
- Egypt, East Africa, Southern Arabia, and SE Asia (*Shafi'i*)

Shi'a
- Iran
- Iraq Majority

Sufism and Mysticism (Tasawuf)

Brotherhoods (*Tariqa*)
- *Alawiyya*
- *Chistiyya*
- *Naqshbandiyya*
- *Qadiriyya*
- *Khalwatiyya*
- *Rifa'iyya*
- *Sammaniyya*
- *Shattariyya*
- *Shadhiliyya*
- *Wujudiyya*

Prevalent Sufi Beliefs
- *Barakah* (Blessing)
- *Keramat* (Holy, Saintly Miracle)
- *Waliyy* (God's friend)
- *Ziyarat* (Grave visitation)

Extreme Sufi Beliefs
- *Fana* (Passing away of self)
- *Dhikr* ("Remembrance," songs, mantras)
- *Wajd* (Trance-like state)

GLOSSARY

Abangan – Javanese "red," which refers to cultural or nominal Muslims in Java.

Abbasid – One of the greatest Islamic dynasties, based out of Baghdad in the 8th century.

Andalusia – Muslim Spain.

Ahmadiyah – A sect of Islam that believes there was another prophet after Muhammad.

Ashari – A semi-rationalist school of thought in early Islam which heavily influenced Shafi'i.

Awliya – Friend of God.

Barakah – Blessing or power from a Muslim saint's gravesite.

Butuni – Arabic for "stomach" or "womb," origin of the name of the island of Buton.

Dhikr – "Remembrance," songs, mantras, or a trancelike state in Sufism.

Dhimmi – Second class citizens in Islamic states, such as Christians and Zoroastrians.

Dukun – A shaman or healer in Indonesia.

Fana – The state of "annihilation" or "passing away of self" pursued by some Sufis.

Fiqh – Islamic jurisprudence.

Hadith – The sayings of and about Muhammad recorded by his companions.

Hajj – The pilgrimage of a Muslim to Mecca and Medina according to tradition.

Hanafi – School of Jurisprudence in Turkey.

Hanbali – School of Jurisprudence in Saudi Arabia.

Haqiqa – Reality or Truth, often the heart of things in Sufism.

Ijma – Consensus.

Ijtihad – Interpretation or independent legal reasoning.

Ilmu – Secret esoteric knowledge.

Iqtida – Imitation of Muhammad's example.

Jihad – struggle or violence in the name of Islam.

Kalam – Theology or Word in Islam.

Keramat – Sacred or Holy site.

Kiai – Javanese term for a charismatic leader, usually in traditional Sufi Islam.

Mahabarata – Epic story from India.

Majapahit – Thirteenth to Sixteenth Century Buddhist kingdom based on the island of Java.

Malamatiyya – "Path of Blame" movement.

Mazhab (or *Madhhab*) – A school of Islamic jurisprudence.

Mutazila – A school of thought in early Islam that uses reason to interpret revelation.

Mukjizat – Miracle.

Maliki – School of Jurisprudence in Northern Africa.

Mughal – Former Islamic Empire based in India.

Muwahhid – Affirmer of unity.

Pata Polena – Term from Buton meaning "life is in ideas."

Pir – The equivalent of a Shakyh or Sufi teacher in India.

Pribumi – Someone from a people group native to the islands of Indonesia.

Quran – "Recitation," the Muslim holy book.

Ramayana – An ancient, important cultural story from India.

Rifa'iyya – A Sufi Brotherhood known for emphasizing wonders and extreme behavior.

Safavid – A Shi'a empire that arose in Iran after the fall of the Persian Empire.

Salafi – Ancestors, the belief that Islamic authority is only in Quran and Hadiths.

Sama – Singing together in Sufi Islam.

Sayyid – A blood descendent of Muhammad.

Shahnameh – The Book of Kings from the Persian Empire.

Shahada – The phrase "There is no God but Allah, and Muhammad is His prophet."

Shariah – Islamic moral law.

Shafi'i – School of Jurisprudence in Yemen, East Africa, and Asia.

Shaykh (or *Sheik*, *Sheikh*, *Syekh*, or *Syek*) – A Sufi teacher and/or head of a brotherhood.

Shi'a – Primarily in Iran and Iraq, Muslims that say first Caliph was uncle of Muhammad.

Shura – Consultation.

Sriwijaya – Eighth to Twelfth Century Buddhist kingdom on Sumatra.

Sufi – Muslims concerned with the heart and spiritual matters, Popular and Orthodox versions.

Sultan – A Muslim king.

Sunna – The context of life during Muhammad's time as passed down in tradition.

Sunni – Muslims who say first Caliphs were Muhammad's companions, over 90% of Muslims.

Taqlid – The conformity of one Muslim to the teaching of another Muslim.

Tariqa (or *Tarekat*) – Sufi Islamic Brotherhood.

Tasawuf – Mysticism or Sufism in Islam.

Tauhid – Unity of Allah.

Ulama – The elite scholars of Islam that can interpret law with authority.

Umayyad – The first Islamic Empire based out of Damascus.

Umma – The body of believers worldwide in Islam.

Wahhabi – A very conservative Islamic school of thought based in Saudi Arabia.

Wahhid – The One.

Wajd – A trance-like state.

Walaya – Friendship with God.

Waliyy – God's friend.

Wujudiyya – Sufi belief that individuals can achieve oneness with Allah, Monism.

Ziyarat – Going to the gravesite of a Muslim saint to pray.

INDEX

A
Abangan 11, 35, 37, 89, 90, 91, 105, 115,
Abbasid 13, 31, 32, 41, 42, 58, 61, 113, 115
Aceh 41, 46, 47, 50, 51, 73, 81, 83, 113
Ambon 19, 49, 50, 54
Arwah 78, 94

B
Baghdad 13, 14, 31, 32, 42, 58, 61, 113, 115
Barakah 70, 90, 114, 115
Baubau 16, 20, 21, 22, 23, 24, 100, 113
Byzantine 29, 32, 33, 61, 113

C
Cairo 7, 17

D
Damascus 29, 30, 31, 113, 118
Demak 47, 48, 113
Dhikr 15, 77, 88, 98, 114, 115

F
Fatimid 33

G
Goa 51, 54
Gowa 54
Gujarat 41, 42, 43, 50, 51, 52, 60, 73, 74, 81, 93

H
Hadhramaut 42, 79, 86
Hajj 13, 85, 86, 116
Hurgronje, Snouck 87, 88

I
Ilmu 91, 99, 116

J
Johor 17, 47, 52, 93

K
Kalam 73, 86, 116
Keramat 15, 70, 98, 114, 116

L
Lapandewa 20, 21, 22

M
Makassar 5, 16, 19, 54
Malabar 40, 41, 43, 73, 108
Malacca 23, 34, 41, 43, 45, 47, 48, 49, 50, 113
Mamluk 33, 42, 113
Martabat Tujuh v, 75, 76, 78, 92, 95, 96, 108
Mongols 32, 42, 61
Morocco 29, 30, 58, 104
Mughal 33, 34, 40, 62, 63, 64, 65, 82, 113, 117
Muhammadiyah 7, 8, 10, 110
Murhum 24, 52, 93

N
Nahdlatul Ulama 10

O
Ottoman 32, 33, 61, 62, 65, 89, 113

S
Safavid 33, 61, 62, 113, 117
Salafi 8, 9, 98, 105, 117
Sayyid 42, 86, 117
Shariah 36, 61, 67, 72, 76, 79, 118
Shaykh 71, 75, 79, 87, 89, 98, 99, 118

T
Tariqa 14, 71, 76, 78, 88, 89, 114, 118
Tasawuf 12, 16, 24, 94, 95, 109, 111, 114, 118
Timurid 63

U
Umayyad 29, 30, 31, 113, 118

W
Wahid, Abdul 16, 17, 22, 23, 24, 25, 52, 93
Wolio 23, 80, 95, 97
Wujudiyya 81, 83, 95, 114, 119

Z
Ziyarat 70, 114, 119

www.ingramcontent.com/pod-product-compliance
Lightning Source LLC
Chambersburg PA
CBHW070607050426
42450CB00011B/3010